The ANCIENT SOUTHWEST

A Guide to Archaeological Sites

GREGORY McNAMEE

Photographs by LARRY LINDAHL

FRONT COVER: *Tonto National Monument, designated in 1907, stands in a once-remote corner of east-central Arizona overlooking what is now Roosevelt Lake. The cliff dwellings there were constructed by members of the little-known but fascinating Salado Culture.*
FULL TITLE PAGE: *Spruce Tree House, Mesa Verde National Park, Colorado.*
RIGHT: *In Dry Fork Canyon, Utah, a Fremont Culture petroglyph contrasts human-made art with an abstract pattern of colorful lichen.*
PAGE V: *This polychrome pot found in Mesa Verde National Park was made some 600 miles away near present Chihuahua, Mexico, in about 1060.*
PAGE VI–VII: *The Great Gallery, found in Canyonlands National Park, Utah, is a trove of significant rock art.*

Rio Nuevo Publishers®
P. O. Box 5250
Tucson, AZ 85703-0250
(520) 623-9558, www.rionuevo.com

Text © 2014 by Gregory McNamee
Photographs © 2004–2014 by Larry Lindahl

Book design: David Jenney Design

Printed in Korea.

10 9 8 7 6 5 4 3 2

Library of Congress Cataloging-in-Publication Data

McNamee, Gregory.
  The ancient southwest : a guide to archaeological sites /
Gregory McNamee ; photographs by Larry Lindahl.
      pages cm
ISBN 978-1-933855-88-2 (pbk.) — ISBN 1-933855-88-6 (pbk.)
1. Indians of North America—Southwest, New—
Antiquities—Guidebooks. 2. Southwest, New—
Antiquities—Guidebooks. I. Lindahl, Larry, photographer.
II. Title.
  E78.S7M39 2014
  979'.01—dc23   2014014906

Photographer's Note

Significant appreciation is given to Vince Kontny for contributing financially to my journey of photographing the Ancient Southwest. A sincere thank you to Gayle Taylor and the Larry Taylor Memorial Fund, Jerry Ehrhardt and June Freden, Bruce and Janet Misamore, Kathy Dunham, Jackie Klieger, James and Sarah Dolliver, Gandolfa Stegmann, David and Margaret Peterson, Ron Krug, Randy and Milton Crewse, Jack and Marlene Conklin, and Dan Gitter, for assistance with the costs of interstate travel, park entry fees, tour fees, guide fees, commercial photography permits, and the expenses of aerial photography.

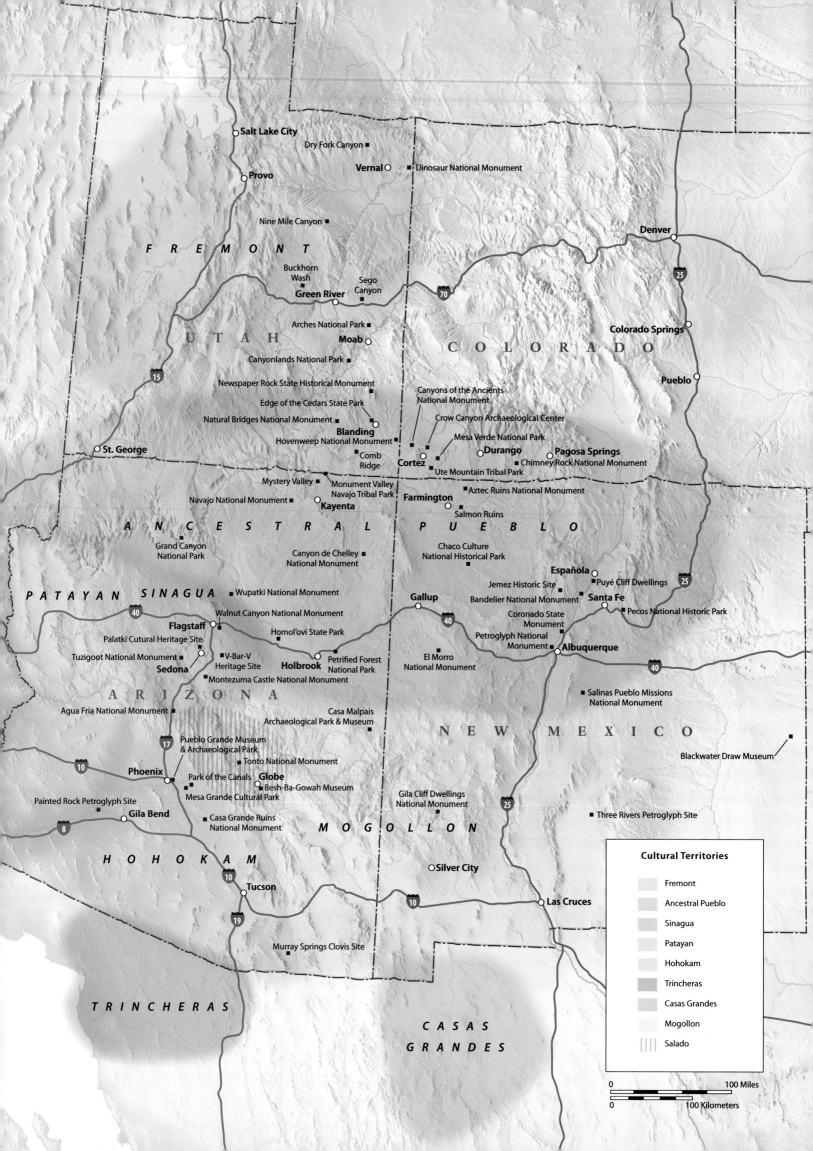

Salt Lake City

Dry Fork Canyon

Vernal • Dinosaur National Monument

Provo

Nine Mile Canyon

F R E M O N T

Denver

25

Buckhorn
Wash
Sego
Canyon
Green River

70

U T A H

Arches National Park

Moab

C O L O R A D O

Colorado Springs

Canyonlands National Park

Pueblo

15

Newspaper Rock State Historical Monument

Canyons of the Ancients
National Monument

Edge of the Cedars State Park

Crow Canyon Archaeological Center

Natural Bridges National Monument

Mesa Verde National Park

Blanding

Durango

Pagosa Springs

St. George

Hovenweep National Monument

Comb
Ridge

Chimney Rock National Monument

Cortez

Ute Mountain Tribal Park

Mystery Valley

Monument Valley
Navajo Tribal Park

Aztec Ruins National Monument

Navajo National Monument

Farmington

A N C E S T R A L   P U E B L O

Kayenta

Salmon Ruins

Grand Canyon
National Park

Canyon de Chelley
National Monument

Chaco Culture
National Historical Park

P A T A Y A N   S I N A G U A

Wupatki National Monument

Española

Puyé Cliff Dwellings

25

Jemez Historic Site

Gallup

Santa Fe

40

Bandelier National Monument

Walnut Canyon National Monument

Coronado State
Monument

Pecos National Historic Park

Flagstaff

Homol'ovi State Park

40

Palatki Cutural Heritage Site

Petroglyph National
Monument

Albuquerque

Tuzigoot National Monument

V-Bar-V
Heritage Site

Petrified Forest
National Park

El Morro
National Monument

40

Sedona

Holbrook

Montezuma Castle National Monument

A R I Z O N A

Salinas Pueblo Missions
National Monument

Agua Fria National Monument

Casa Malpais
Archaeological Park & Museum

N E W   M E X I C O

Pueblo Grande Museum
& Archaeological Park

17

Tonto National Monument

Blackwater Draw Museum

10

Park of the Canals

Globe

Phoenix

Besh-Ba-Gowah Museum

Gila Cliff Dwellings
National Monument

25

Mesa Grande Cultural Park

Painted Rock Petroglyph Site

Casa Grande Ruins
National Monument

Three Rivers Petroglyph Site

Gila Bend

8

M O G O L L O N

H O H O K A M

Silver City

Cultural Territories	
	Fremont
	Ancestral Pueblo
	Sinagua
	Patayan
	Hohokam
	Trincheras
	Casas Grandes
	Mogollon
	Salado

10

Tucson

19

Murray Springs Clovis Site

Las Cruces

10

T R I N C H E R A S

C A S A S
G R A N D E S

0   100 Miles

0   100 Kilometers

Contents

These…supernatural figures…hover in space…
faceless but some stare back at you with large,
hollow disquieting eyes…beware, traveler,
you are approaching the land of the horned gods….

—EDWARD ABBEY, *Desert Solitaire*

THE GREAT GALLERY

BY LARRY LINDAHL

The sandy trail leading up Horseshoe Canyon offers soft footing, slowing the pace, quieting my steps. Along the canyon floor, cottonwood trees shimmer with fantastically bright yellow leaves below pastel sandstone cliffs, and a shallow, meandering creek glistens and sparkles under the deep-blue autumn sky.

After driving a thirty-one-mile dirt road from the highway, then descending a 750-foot cliff down switchbacks into the canyon, a three-and-a-half-mile trail then takes me to the most revered pictograph panel in the entire American Southwest. Photos I had seen show a majestic, otherworldly grouping of ghostly figures spread two hundred feet across that appear to float above the canyon floor. The twenty or more life-size figures were painted more than one thousand years ago.

Along the trail, small collections of pictographs appear up on the cliffs and hidden in caves. In the back of one enormously large alcove, I discover a series of roughly painted pictographs on the pale-peach sandstone. They sit low to the ground in faded red, gray, and brown. Sounds in this space seem to float and shift.

In the middle of the alcove, I sing a sustained single note into the curved stone ceiling. As I fine-tune the pitch, duration, and direction, it creates a new pattern of resonance. With subtle nuances, I soon find an unexpected moment when my voice starts to harmonically resonate with its echo. The energizing sound washes over everything, and the sustained reverberations penetrate deep inside me. The sandstone cavern seems to come alive. I head out to once again find the trail, and traversing a narrow gap in the canyon, I hear sounds of my passage gently echo and then vanish.

After hiking a few hours, I walk around another bend in the canyon, and there, at a distance, I see the creation of an ancient artist. The sheer size of the figures draws me forward. Majestic, yes. Magical. Mysterious, too.

On a particular day, this tall canyon wall was like a blank canvas ready to receive the artist's idea. In that initial application of paint, the rusty-red pigment began to tell a powerful, yet silent story. I wonder where the artist's moist paintbrush first touched the cliff wall to begin this over-sized masterpiece.

A young family arrives at the site. Then, a retirement-age couple walks up. We all take cover from the bright sun under a few small cottonwood trees. The older man pulls binoculars from his daypack, and soon delights in discovering barely perceptible details in the rock art. He shares the binoculars for each of us to see. Through the binoculars I see a row of tiny, incised marks that look like fringe across the chest of one figure's attire. Small white dots, surprising accents of turquoise, and faint incised patterns also reveal nuances undistinguished by the naked eye. The detail within the figures is astounding.

All of our conversations fade to an attentive hush when flute music begins drifting down the canyon. Expressive notes float and echo along, reappear softer and quieter, and then finally dance away. My friend Ron Ayers has hiked farther up the canyon and is playing an improvised melody from his wooden flute. In each breath, his music brushes around the canyon corner, haunting and beautiful.

Ron eventually returns to the curious gathering of hikers sharing time in the wilderness. Heart-felt thanks are given for his gift to us, and among the compliments, he appreciates an offering of chocolate. The artist of the ancient glyphs will, however, miss the audience's response to his mysterious paintings. How do we say thank you? I hope sincere gratitude is truly enough.

Introduction

THE ANCIENT SOUTHWEST

In December 2013, archaeologists from Britain's University of Durham announced that they had identified the oldest human footprints yet found in North America. Discovered in a place called Cuatro Ciénagas (Four Marshes) in the Mexican state of Chihuahua, which borders New Mexico and Texas, those footprints are more than 10,500 years old, predating the next-oldest set of footprints in North America by more than 5,000 years.

In the 1970s, when I was an anthropology student at the University of Arizona, the orthodox view was that humans had walked from Asia across the Bering Sea land bridge precisely ten thousand years ago. (In archaeological convention, this would be rendered either 10,000 BP, or years before the present, or 8,000 BCE, before the common or current era, BCE and CE replacing the older BC and AD.) From an entry point in Alaska, these first peoples had then fanned out across the North American continent, eventually working their way to Panama and onward to South America.

Our view is considerably complicated today, five decades later. The oldest known human print in the Americas, a child's footprint dating to 13,000 BP, was found in Chile. Archaeologists have proposed a date for a newly discovered rock art site near Las Vegas, Nevada, at 14,000 BP, while others have maintained that archaeological sites near the Rio Grande in southern New Mexico date to as early as 25,000 BP. Controversies are plentiful and agreements rare, but each generation of archaeologists, as they acquire new information and advance new interpretations, has pushed the chronology

of human habitation in the Americas ever further back in time.

This book is a journey into the ancient past of the Southwest, focusing on national and state parks, monuments, and other sites that have shed light on such questions as when and where the first peoples arrived in the region, what they did and made while they flourished here, when they began to grow corn and other important food crops, and where they went when the three main cultures of the ancient Southwest—the Hohokam, Ancestral Pueblo, and Mogollon—dispersed about seven hundred years ago. As we travel through the Southwest and visit these sites, we will ask other questions: What did the early peoples who lived in the Southwest know about the sky above? What is the meaning of the art—pottery, pictographs, petroglyphs—that they left behind? What techniques did they use to build structures that have lasted hundreds of years? What compelled them to build vast cities such as Chaco Canyon, and why did they suddenly leave their homes?

To answer these and many other questions, archaeologists make inferences from evidence—the structures that cultures leave behind, as well as garbage middens, burial sites, works of art, and other artifacts—and "ethnographic analogy," which means looking at the lifeways and beliefs of people who have lived within the historical record for clues about the more distant past. Many modern peoples in the Southwest, for instance, consider their homelands to be bounded by sacred mountains; does this suggest that the ancient peoples did as well? Pueblo stories tell of a time when Coyote,

Above: Ancient hunters used tools such as these shaped bones, found in Aztec Ruins National Monument, New Mexico, to scrape hides.

Opposite: A series of doorways in Aztec Ruins National Monument, New Mexico, admits sunlight deep within an ancient pueblo.

Above: Attributed to Hohokam makers, this arrowhead was found in the Sinagua pueblo known as Tuzigoot National Monument, Arizona.

Opposite: Ceramics, such as these displayed at Keet Seel, Navajo National Monument, Arizona, indicate that a site was permanently settled because ceramics are less easily transported than the woven baskets migratory peoples usually use.

a trickster found in the folklore of people throughout North America, had a human form until he was punished for committing one transgression too many. The O'odham people tell stories of a great flood that destroyed much of their world. These stories are all very old, stretching into antiquity, so far back that it is reasonable to suppose that the people of this dry, austere region have told them from the very beginning.

In this book, we define that region as what some archaeologists and historians have called the "core Southwest," taking in all of the modern states of Arizona and New Mexico, along with eastern Utah and southwestern Colorado. The text is organized by state. Archaeologists debate whether to include southeastern California and southwestern Texas, and many consider northern Mexico—including the Cuatro Ciénagas site where those ancient footprints were found—to belong to the Southwest as well. Our travels here will take us only to sites within that core region—more than fifty major sites in all.

THE PEOPLES OF THE ANCIENT SOUTHWEST

The First Peoples

We know that people have been in the Southwest for a very long time—certainly more than thirteen thousand years, and probably far earlier than that. When they arrived, they found a very different place from the one that we have today. The Sonoran Desert, the homeland of the O'odham, Hohokam, and Salado peoples, was carpeted with ponderosa pine, alligator juniper, and other plants now found much higher in elevation. The annual rainfall in the lowlands was more than forty inches, about the level Iowa now receives, and the mountains received nearly twice that amount. The land was the province of large animals that have since disappeared, many of which offered quite a larder for the Paleoindians, as archaeologists call the first peoples here.

The earliest tradition that archaeologists have documented well is called the Clovis Culture, which dates to about 13,000 BP—but whose dates, as we have already noted, are being steadily pushed back to an even

earlier time. Throughout the Southwest, at places such as the Murray Springs Clovis Site in southeastern Arizona (see page 13), archaeologists have found the remains of mammoths, a favorite prey of Clovis hunters. At Blackwater Draw, in northeastern New Mexico (see page 51), first excavated in 1929, the remains of other animals that would soon become extinct, including the smilodon (sabertooth cat) and dire wolf, have turned up alongside weapons clearly made by human hunters.

On the night of August 27, 1908, a torrential rain began to fall on the small town of Folsom, in the northeastern corner of New Mexico. The Cimarron River, which cut across a nearby mesa, soon overflowed its banks, and floodwaters gouged deep into the washes that fed into them. Folsom was destroyed, and seventeen people died. Surveying the damage, an African American cowboy named George McJunkin wandered into a place called Wild Horse Arroyo, which had been deepened ten feet by the flood, and found a pile of bison bones, clearly very old, that were larger than those of modern bison. He also found a pile of intricately worked projectile points, different enough from those of the Clovis Culture that archaeologists designated the people who made them the Folsom Culture, which dates to about 11,000 BP. At Ventana Cave, in southwestern Arizona, archaeologist Emil Haury catalogued evidence of the protein-rich diet of the people of that time: the bones of prairie dogs, otters, camels, short-faced bears, deer, badgers, wolves, jaguars, horses, and bison lay intermingled with scrapers, flint projectile points, and choppers.

Over time, other traditions evolved from these Clovis and Folsom forebears. Archaeologists name their time the "Archaic era," and it is to this long span that we can trace the origins of the Ancestral Pueblo, Hohokam, Fremont, Mogollon, and other regional cultures, the makers of the sites we will visit in this book.

The Ancestral Pueblo People

On a winter morning in 1888, a rancher named Richard Wetherill went searching for a lost calf deep in a winding canyon on the Colorado Plateau, not far from the point

where three territories and a state joined to form what is now the Four Corners. Descending into a draw so steep that his horse could not follow, he stumbled upon an astonishing find: a large cliff house that seemed almost to hang in midair before a sheer, high sandstone wall. In the ruin, one of many in what is now Mesa Verde National Park, Wetherill and a fellow cowboy found baskets, pots, and preserved grains and ears of corn that lay out on wooden benches as if ready to be eaten. It was, he recalled, almost as if its occupants had been chased away in the middle of a meal.

The discovery excited the attention of generations of archaeologists. Through their work, much is now known about the people once called "Anasazi," a Navajo phrase that is often translated as "the enemies of our ancestors." Naturally, the descendants of those people—who form a group of tribes and nations called the Pueblo people, named after the house structure that so many of them retained from ancient times—dislike their forebears being called the enemy, and the term most archaeologists use today is "Ancestral Pueblo."

The Ancestral Pueblo people, archaeologists think, comprised a blend of migrants from central Mexico and elsewhere in the Southwest, along with descendants of the "Basketmaker" peoples who had lived in the Colorado Plateau country for thousands of years. For the most part, the early Ancestral Puebloans lived in small settlements, most now lost to time. About two thousand years ago, those settlements began to take on a somewhat more permanent nature, marked by pithouses—structures dug partway into the ground like shallow basements and then covered with wood and dirt. Somewhat more permanent, we say, because these settlements, often accommodating only members of a single family or clan, were usually vacated after only ten or twenty years, sometimes reoccupied by other groups in search of good farming and hunting ground.

By 500 CE, these people were living in complex pithouses, most of them in scattered locations near hunting grounds and fields in places such as Cedar Mesa, Utah,

Stone Tools

In the game of rock-paper-scissors, when rock meets rock, neither player is declared the winner, and the game begins anew. In the life of a user of stone tools, when rock meets rock, the stronger chips away at the weaker, and in time a good hammerstone—usually a river cobble of hard stone, fitted to a hand—will turn an undifferentiated piece of flint, chert, or obsidian into a projectile point or knife that can bring down game or skin a carcass.

The ancient peoples of the Southwest put a premium on well-made stone tools, or lithics, that flew straight and true, cut well, and could be used to make other tools: spears, arrows, axes, knives, hammers, and grinders. They gathered materials from sites that produced particularly good stone, such as Florida Mountain south of the Mimbres Valley of south-central New Mexico, where an ancient quarry yielded andesite, rhyolite, chert, quartzite, and obsidian, the last a kind of volcanic glass that was especially favored for its durability and the sharp point it kept.

It is tempting, when visiting a site where ancient people lived, to see an arrowhead in every piece of rock on the ground. Often natural processes will break chert and flint into shapes that look as if they had been knapped, or chipped into tools. Often, too, erosion and time will break away shaped tools so that they appear to be mere rocks. It takes a practiced eye to tell which is which.

and the San Juan River valley of northern New Mexico. Two centuries passed, and surface pueblos began to appear, pithouses now taking the form of kivas, subterranean structures that served both practical and ceremonial purposes and almost certainly helped reinforce the customs and beliefs of local communities in important ways.

More than a thousand years ago, the Ancestral Pueblo people began to build large cities, marked by multifamily dwellings, public structures called great houses, many kivas, and large public plazas that would have been the site of spectacular rituals. Great communities such as Chaco Canyon (see pages 55–57), some with many thousands of inhabitants, began to form, connected by roads and social interactions. With the rise of urbanism, these Ancestral Pueblo settlements were occupied for centuries.

Above: Bound with cord and twine, a stone ax found at Mesa Verde National Park, Colorado, retains its original handle.

Opposite: The Cliff Palace at Mesa Verde National Park, Colorado, is one of the greatest cultural treasures of the American Southwest.

The Chaco settlement ended in about 1130, for reasons that may have to do with drought, resulting famine, and perhaps warfare or, as some archaeologists believe, religious or political dissension. In the years that followed, the Ancestral Pueblo people tended to live in pueblos and cliff dwellings, and they would do so for another century or two in places such as Mesa Verde and Betatakin. Then they left. Not long after those places were vacated, new peoples began to enter the region, including the Navajo—and, not long after them, the Spanish, and with them the beginning of written history.

The Fremont Culture

Named for the Fremont River, which flows through central Utah to an eventual confluence with the Colorado River, the people of the Fremont Culture inhabited a vast area of deserts and mountains to the northwest of the Ancestral Puebloans, taking in much of Utah and parts of Nevada and Colorado. The forerunners of the Fremont people had lived in this country for untold thousands of years, but a distinctive Fremont tradition began at about 700 CE and endured until about 1300, the time of the collapse of the "big three" cultures to the south.

The Fremont people are best known today for their petroglyphs and pictographs, rock art that is an integral part of any visit to places such as Dinosaur National Monument (see page 76) and Canyonlands National Park (see pages 77–78). Unlike their neighbors, though, they tended not to build monumental architecture or live in cities, instead preferring to live in small, probably family-governed settlements along watercourses, where they grew subsistence-level crops of beans, corn, and other food plants.

Many archaeologists believe that the Fremont people were among the ancestors of the modern Ute and Shoshone peoples.

The Hohokam

Like the Ancestral Puebloans, the people who settled in the river valleys and low

Below: Buffalo hunters are depicted in a diorama at Mesa Verde National Park.

Chronology of the Ancient Southwest

BEFORE 11,000 BCE	9,500 BCE	8,000 BCE	ANCESTRAL PUEBLO CULTURE	
Humans arrive in the Southwest	Clovis Culture emerges	Folsom Culture emerges	**6500–300 BCE** Archaic Period Colorado Plateau: Basketmaker I, Early (6500–1200 BCE), Basketmaker I, Late (1200 BCE–1 CE) Desert Lowlands: Cochise Culture (6500–300 BCE)	**300 BCE–550 CE** Colorado Plateau: Basketmaker II (1–500 CE) Desert Lowlands: Pioneer Hohokam (300 BCE–550 CE) Mogollon Highlands: Early Pithouse Mogollon (200–550 CE)

country of southern and central Arizona lived in small villages made up of pithouses and grew crops alongside streams, gathering wild foods—such as mesquite beans and saguaro fruits—and hunting to add to their diet. Over time, these early people learned to harness the waters of the desert and began to build canals that enabled them to control the flow of water to their fields, growing irrigated crops such as corn and beans as early as 2100 BCE.

An increasingly complex pottery tradition went hand in hand with this development, allowing them to store food securely for future use, as well as to cook stews and other soft foods that, among other things, allowed Hohokam mothers to wean their babies earlier, freeing themselves for other work. These innovations enabled the farmers, in a sense, to sidestep the desert's natural cycle of aridity and famine, providing surplus foods in time of want. Over centuries, the Hohokam developed a material culture that is among the richest in all of North America, as evidenced by great cities such as Casa Grande (see pages 13–15) and Snaketown, both lying near the Gila River in south-central Arizona.

Archaeologists have argued over the origins of the Hohokam for decades. One once-influential school holds that the people migrated as a group north from Mexico, and there are some traits that the Hohokam share with Mesoamerican cultures, such as pottery styles and motifs and the overhanging-end grinding stones called manos. However, it now seems likely that the ancestors of the Hohokam gradually developed from the earlier hunting-and-gathering peoples of the region after a long-term drought began to abate some four thousand years ago. Migrants from Mesoamerica may have joined them, traders from the south certainly visited them, and some cultural features were influenced by Mesoamerican sources, but the development of Hohokam civilization seems for now to be a largely indigenous phenomenon.

Below: This black-on-white olla, made by an Ancestral Pueblo potter in the late 11th or 12th century, was found nearly intact at Wupatki, a Sinagua settlement near what is now Flagstaff, Arizona.

1530s

First European contact

500–1100

Colorado Plateau:
Basketmaker III (500–700);
Pueblo I (700–900);
Pueblo II (900–1100),
during which Chaco Canyon flourishes
Fremont Culture emerges in southern Utah (700)

Desert Lowlands:
Colonial Hohokam (500–900);
Sedentary Hohokam (900–1100)

Mogollon Highlands:
Late Pithouse Mogollon (550–1000 CE)

1100–1450

Regionwide droughts,
1130–1180, 1275–1300

Colorado Plateau:
Pueblo III (1100–1300),
when Hovenweep and Mesa Verde become major sites

Desert Lowlands:
Classic Hohokam Period (1100–1450);
Casa Grande completed (1350)

Mogollon Highlands:
Mimbres Mogollon Period (1100–1450)

Sinagua Culture:
Wupatki founded (1120),
Tuzigoot founded (1125);
Montezuma Castle predominates
southern Sinagua region (1300–1450)

The great Hohokam cities, many located in or near what are now metropolitan Phoenix and Tucson, dwindled about the time the Ancestral Pueblo people vacated theirs. The very name Hohokam comes from the Akimel O'odham (River People) phrase meaning something like "those who have finished." Those Hohokam cities may have been vacated, but the people did not disappear. Instead, they live on in the O'odham who have made southern Arizona and the Mexican state of Sonora their home for centuries. Some Hopi and Zuni clans also trace ancestry to the Hohokam past.

The Mogollon

Thousands of years ago, people from the desert lowlands made their way into the mountain country near the headwaters of the Gila River, in southwestern New Mexico. Called the Cochise Culture after the great (but ethnically unrelated) Apache leader of the nineteenth century, these early people grew corn, squash, and other crops acquired from traders who traveled along the Sierra Madre to the south, carrying goods from Mexico.

As they developed a farming tradition, the Cochise people settled permanently along streams and rivers in the rugged mountain country, evolving into what archaeologists now call the Mogollon Culture. In the mature stages of their culture, the Mogollon, and particularly the branch known today as the Mimbres (a Spanish word for "willow," given to another river that flows out of the Gila highlands), were renowned for the black-on-white painted pottery they made of riverbank clay, examples of which have been found as far south as central Mexico and as far west as the Pacific coast of California. Potters throughout the Southwest emulated Mimbres styles, though with variations that allow archaeologists to distinguish among different traditions.

The Mogollon people dominated the highlands and Mimbres Valley until about 1300 CE, when drought and perhaps warfare led to the eventual disintegration of their classic culture, the hallmark site of which is the Gila Cliff Dwellings National Monument (see pages 51–52). Archaeologists believe that some southern Mogollon people moved into the Sierra Madre, becoming the ancestors of today's Tarahumara, while northern Mogollon people were among the ancestors of today's Zuni and Hopi people.

The Sinagua

When Spanish explorers first arrived in the area of what is now Flagstaff, Arizona, and beheld the state's tallest mountains, the San Francisco Peaks, they were mystified that great rivers did not flow from them. They accordingly gave the mountains the name "Sierra sin Agua," or "mountain range without water." Archaeologist Harold Colton borrowed the term centuries later to describe the people of the area, who, he argued, formed a culture separate from the Ancestral Pueblo people to the east and the Hohokam to the south.

The Sinagua probably migrated from the Mojave Desert in the west into the high country in about 500 CE and then built pithouses, an architectural form that they borrowed from their new neighbors. In time, again borrowing from the Ancestral Puebloans, they began to construct large surface pueblos made of tightly fitted stone and adobe. Toward the end of their life as a distinctive culture, the Sinagua built the cliff dwelling of Montezuma Castle (see pages 36–37) in the Verde Valley of Arizona, a site resembling Ancestral Pueblo cliff dwellings in places such as Betatakin and Mesa Verde.

Archaeologists group the Sinagua into two branches: the Northern Sinagua, who lived in the area of Flagstaff, and the Southern Sinagua, who settled along the Verde River. Over time, these groups took on slightly different traits in architecture, weaving, pottery making, and other pursuits, but contact among them was steady and, to all appearances, friendly. That was not so of contact with a group of new arrivals, also migrants from the western desert, the ancestors of the modern Yavapai Indians, against whom, the archaeological evidence suggests, the Sinagua were in conflict in their final years as a distinct culture.

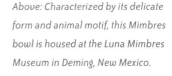

Above: Characterized by its delicate form and animal motif, this Mimbres bowl is housed at the Luna Mimbres Museum in Deming, New Mexico.

Opposite: Wukoki Pueblo, on the Colorado Plateau of northern Arizona, is one of the most important sites of the ancient Sinagua Culture.

The Salado

The Salado Culture, which flourished from about 1150 until about 1450, arose in the Tonto Basin of east-central Arizona and eventually spread south into the Superstition Mountains east of metropolitan Phoenix and the area around present-day Globe. Archaeologists initially considered the Salado to be a Hohokam population, and some hold to that opinion today, with the proviso that the Salado absorbed many more Ancestral Pueblo and Mogollon traits than did the Hohokam to the west and south. By all evidence, for instance, the Salado did not make use of the ballcourts that were so important to classical Hohokam society, but neither did they build kivas, unlike the Ancestral Puebloans and Mogollon.

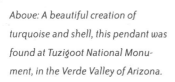

The Salado people were masters at building multistory pueblos and, later, cliff dwellings such as those found at Tonto National Monument (see pages 37–41). In this respect they were like the Ancestral Pueblo and Mogollon peoples, but they made extensive use of adobe, like the Hohokam. Like the Hohokam, too, they built extensive irrigation networks in the area of what is now Roosevelt Dam. Unlike the Hohokam, though, who mostly cremated their dead, and the Ancestral Pueblo and Mogollon peoples, who often buried their dead under the floors of the houses where they had lived, the Salado buried their dead in areas set aside for that purpose—cemeteries, in other words. They often left goods such as jewelry and ceramics, including the polychrome pottery for which they are justly renowned, in the graves of the departed.

When the Salado Culture collapsed, some of its members likely moved south to Casas Grandes in what is now Chihuahua, Mexico. Some may have moved north, joining Ancestral Pueblo people as they moved eastward into the Rio Grande Valley.

Above: A beautiful creation of turquoise and shell, this pendant was found at Tuzigoot National Monument, in the Verde Valley of Arizona.

Opposite: At least 3,000 years old, the Head of Sinbad pictograph panel is attributed to the Barrier Canyon Culture of southern Utah.

VISITING THE ANCIENT SOUTHWEST

"Take only memories, leave only footprints," runs the old hiker's motto. Of a visit to any archaeological site in the Southwest, we might add "photographs" to what to take and "donations" to what to leave, but the general principle holds true. Although they have endured for centuries, these archaeological sites are fragile, so please remember to leave all objects—even the smallest pebble—in place. Photograph or draw any artifacts or structures that you find interesting, but do not remove them from the site. Do not stand, sit, or climb on ancient walls or foundations, and stay on established trails or paths. And as much as we all love our dogs, they can cause unintentional damage to a site—so leave them at home, at the hotel, or at the campsite. (For more on "archaeological etiquette," visit the Society for American Archaeology web site, www.saa.org.)

Many archaeological sites in the Southwest lie in remote parts of the region, and some are seldom visited. Be sure to bring food such as granola bars, trail mix, and lightly salted mixed nuts, as well as a couple of gallons of water per person. Check your radiator for water and your tires for air before venturing into areas where cell phones do not work. (As a rule of thumb, assume that they won't work, or will work only spottily, once you're five miles—eight kilometers—from the nearest interstate highway.) If you're going into remote country, let a friend or relative know your itinerary. Whenever possible, even when it's not required to do so, it's a good idea to stop in at a site's visitor center and sign and date the guest log so that there's a record of when you arrived—and, more important, so that you can ask about local road and weather conditions, learn about new discoveries, equip yourself with updated maps and brochures, browse the bookstore and gift shop, and get a better feel for the place.

All those cautions aside, we hope that you will enjoy your explorations of the ancient Southwest, will take many memories, and will leave many footprints.

ARIZONA

MURRAY SPRINGS CLOVIS SITE

» Clovis Culture

Located in the valley of the San Pedro River near Sierra Vista, Arizona, the Murray Springs Clovis Site dates to about 11,000 BCE. There, Clovis hunters attacked and killed a mammoth, a young adult female who fell about forty feet (12 m) from a water hole that mammoths had dug. The archaeologists who discovered and excavated the site found an intact Clovis spear point and three fragments with the remains, while nearby lay butchering tools and thousands of flint flakes, as well as a tool made of mammoth bone that was used to straighten spear shafts—the only tool of its kind ever discovered in the Americas. Hunters from the same culture also killed eleven bison here, members of an extinct Ice Age species.

Murray Springs is a quiet, little-visited place today, yet it is one of the most extensively excavated and most accurately dated Paleoindian sites in North America. It is thus of international importance. As archaeologist Bruce Huckell has remarked, the Murray Springs Clovis Site allows us to "see much, if not all, of the range of implement forms and technological approaches used by a people whose not-so-distant ancestors were born in the Old World." So significant is the site in providing evidence of how these early Americans lived that in 2012 the Murray Springs Clovis Site was designated a National Historic Landmark.

CASA GRANDE RUINS NATIONAL MONUMENT

» Hohokam Culture

When Jesuit missionary Eusebio Francisco Kino first came to the Hohokam structure that he called the Casa Grande, "the great house," at the end of 1694, he likened it to the castles of his homeland. He added that the surrounding ruins suggested that "in ancient times there had been a city here," perhaps even one of the Seven Cities of Cibola that Francisco Vásquez de Coronado (see page 61) had sought.

Those cities abounded in gold, legend had it. Gold was not to be found at Casa Grande, roughly midway between modern-day Phoenix and Tucson. But other treasures were, so much so that in 1892 the Casa Grande Ruins archaeological site, whose main structure was completed in about 1350 CE, was designated the nation's first federally protected archaeological preserve.

Casa Grande, the great house itself, is an impressive structure, four stories high and about sixty feet (18 m) long, made up of more than three thousand tons of caliche (a mixture of sand, clay, and lime) mud. Many of the 640-some beams that ran across the structure, mostly ponderosa pine and fir, probably came from the distant Pinal, Santa Catalina, and Galiuro mountains, transported somehow for at least sixty miles (96 km).

The prehistoric people who lived along the Gila and other rivers did so seasonally, traveling into the desert to collect plant and animal food. Eventually, they began to settle in small villages, characterized by groups of pithouses, used for dwelling and storage, that faced onto each other in small courtyards, suggesting that people who were related to each other lived close together, with other clusters of family compounds at a greater distance. As these settlements grew, these villages became small neighborhoods in a larger city that came to include features

Above: This dog figurine was recovered from a Hohokam settlement in Arizona. Important to every culture in the ancient Southwest, dogs accompanied the first hunters to arrive in the Americas.

Opposite: The "big house" that lends its name to Casa Grande Ruins National Monument is located in the Hohokam heartland near the Gila River of south-central Arizona.

» U.S. Bureau of
Land Management
1763 Paseo San Luis
Sierra Vista, AZ 85635–4611
(520) 439–6400
www.blm.gov/az/st/en/
prog/cultural/murray.html

A thriving town, its structures probably organized along kinship lines, surrounded the Hohokam big house at Casa Grande.

» Casa Grande Ruins
National Monument
1100 Ruins Drive
Coolidge, AZ 85228
(928) 723-3172
www.nps.gov/cagr

such as ballcourts, which are common in settlements established earlier in the area of what is now Mexico City. For this and other reasons, archaeologists trace a connection between Mesoamerica and the Hohokam homeland.

Casa Grande Ruins National Monument contains one such ballcourt, a kind of structure that was popular among the Hohokam from about 800 until about 1070 CE, after which they were no longer built. The "great house" and built-up platform mounds date to a later period that begins at about 1150 CE. Casa Grande is the best-known survivor of all the Hohokam great houses, a combination ceremonial complex, astronomical observatory, storehouse, and elite residence. What is perhaps most interesting about the big building is that, according to chronological evidence provided by tree-ring dating (see page 59) and other techniques, it was built continuously; while many sites in the Southwest, such as Chaco Canyon, required generations to construct, Casa Grande was probably constructed by the same group of people from start to finish. It took them several years, but they built a structure with walls four feet (1.2 m) thick at the base and with a commanding view of the Gila River valley for miles in every direction. No less monumental were the deep canals that irrigated the surrounding fields, bringing water from the river more than a mile away and

distributing it over thousands of acres.

As you enter the compound and plaza that surround the great house, you can see the remains of other structures made, like the great house, of adobe. This plaza served as a public space where religious ceremonies were held, and in some instances where ancestors were buried. In earlier generations of village life, the plaza had been open, but by the time the great house was built, it was ringed by tall walls. Inside those walls, the open family compounds of old, made up of clusters of single structures, were replaced by multifamily buildings and platform mounds, which resemble flat-topped pyramids. All of these structures were brightly painted, adding to their impressive appearance.

From the material that has been recovered at Casa Grande and other nearby sites, fine examples of which are on exhibit at the visitor center, we have a good picture of the Hohokam world a millennium ago. We know that the Hohokam people were fond of jewelry, prizing in particular bracelets made of seashells from the Gulf of California. They cremated or buried their dead, leaving artifacts such as pottery and jewelry in the graves. They traded widely for imported goods such as copper bells and iron mirrors. They enjoyed a varied diet of many kinds of cultivated vegetables, wild plants, and game animals.

We are also left with mysteries, including the origins of the big-house builders. According to archaeologist Jesse Fewkes, Akimel O'odham guides at the Casa Grande excavations he conducted from 1906 to 1908 told him that the great houses were built by a people who came from the north, led by a chief they called El Siba, which means "the bitter man" or "the cruel man." Some archaeologists have suggested that these leaders were from the Salado Culture, others a branch of the Ancestral Pueblo people, but a more plausible version—one favored by some archaeologists as well as the Akimel O'odham and Tohono O'odham who occupied the Gila Valley historically and still today—the Hohokam (known by some experts and tribal members as the Ancient Sonoran Desert People) never left the region but instead just moved around within it and are ancestral to the O'odham who still inhabit southern Arizona today. Today six tribes claim a link to the Great House and surrounding archaeological sites.

PUEBLO GRANDE MUSEUM AND ARCHAEOLOGICAL PARK

» Hohokam Culture

The Casa Grande and its neighbors of Snaketown and Grewe (which are not open to the public) were important Hohokam settlements. However, the Salt River Valley to the north of the Gila River, where metropolitan Phoenix now stands, saw the largest and most densely populated settlements in Hohokam history, with many "great houses" as large as or even larger than the one at the Casa Grande, and many flourishing villages that controlled a huge system of canals that in turn fed vast fields of corn, beans, squash, pumpkins, tobacco, agaves, cotton, and peppers.

Archaeologist Jerry Howard, a specialist in Hohokam irrigation, has estimated that it would have taken the builders a million person-days of labor to build the canals, plus the time required to clear and maintain them once they were in place. Add to that the fact that the Hohokam had a canal-building technology that was limited to stone and wooden digging tools and woven baskets with which to remove soil by hand, and their accomplishment becomes all the more remarkable.

Ancient Pottery

The presence of pottery in an archaeological site tells archaeologists that the people who lived there were settled enough to store grains and other goods in containers that, though durable, were not as easy to transport as woven baskets or cloth sacks. Pottery, in other words, suggests permanent settlements, and throughout the Southwest, pottery begins to appear at the time when nomadic peoples started to settle in villages such as Casa Grande. Early pottery tended to be crudely made, but with time distinctive pottery traditions developed. At Casa Grande, for instance, some pottery was locally made, but the presence of ceramics from distant sources indicates that the Hohokam had developed an extensive trade network.

In the Hohokam ceramic tradition, reddish, buff, or light-brown clays dominate, often painted with red geometric motifs. Most Hohokam ceramics were made by using what potters call the "paddle and anvil" technique, by which the potter holds a tool against the inside of the vessel while striking the outside with a wooden paddle to shape it, which lends the vessel a slightly rough texture.

Above: Made by Hohokam settlers in the Verde Valley of Arizona, this red-on-buff bowl graced a family's quarters at Walnut Canyon National Monument to the north.

A Hohokam redware urn stands alongside an earth-and-stone wall at Pueblo Grande Museum and Archaeological Park. Right: Archaeologists usually find ceramics in the form of fragments, such as these sherds of decorated Hohokam pottery.

» Pueblo Grande Museum
and Archaeological Park
4619 E. Washington Street,
Phoenix, AZ 85034
(602) 495-0901
www.pueblogrande.com

Even under the best of conditions, Hohokam life was difficult. At Pueblo Grande, a large village right next door to present-day Sky Harbor International Airport in Phoenix, excavations uncovered hundreds of graves that showed a high rate of mortality among children and young teenagers. Moreover, very few people there lived beyond the age of fifty, and those who did were often in ill health. Hohokam life in the Classic Period (1150–1450 CE) may have been materially richer than that of earlier times, but it was still far from idyllic.

Pueblo Grande was first settled more than two thousand years ago as a small village of a few clusters of pithouses. Over time, it grew to a village of more than a thousand residents, extending perhaps two miles (3.2 km) along a canal system that ran northwestward from the Salt River. Only a small part of that original community is protected by the Pueblo Grande Museum and Archaeological Park, but that small part—which encompasses only about one-tenth of the original thousand or so acres (405 ha) in the original settlement—is extraordinarily significant, including the remains of a ballcourt and those of a vast earthen platform mound that extends nearly four hundred feet (122 m) across, paved with a surface of caliche mud as durable as concrete.

About a hundred other such mounds have been discovered in the Hohokam world, and their uses have been debated—they may have served as watchtowers, ceremonial structures, or raised foundations for great houses. Whatever its purpose, the platform mound at Pueblo Grande is the largest and best preserved of any known from the Hohokam world, lying within the heart of a huge modern city. That mound and the reconstructed canals and other remains at Pueblo Grande make for a must-see destination for anyone with an interest in the Hohokam past.

By about 1450, the Salt River Valley was essentially depopulated. Archaeologists believe that a number of events caused the Hohokam to leave the Salt River Valley. One was a series of floods in the winter of 1358–59, which destroyed the canals and turned the Hohokam fields into untillable mud flats. Immediately following the flood, a long drought settled in, followed by yet another period of wet weather and flooding. Analysis of graves from this period showed that the people of the region suffered from malnutrition and associated ailments such as osteoporosis and anemia.

PARK OF THE CANALS AND MESA GRANDE CULTURAL PARK

» Hohokam Culture

Remains of the ancient Hohokam canals are scattered throughout the Phoenix area, but the Park of the Canals, located just a mile (1.6 km) from downtown Mesa, offers some of the best-preserved of them. A tour of the small park readily shows how skillful they were in their building techniques. The modern canals that flow along or just a few yards away from where the Hohokam so laboriously dug theirs, bringing irrigation water to the fields of farmers today, are less efficient than the ancient ones in that respect.

Mesa Grande, located near Park of the Canals, is a Hohokam site with a platform mound that is second in size only to that of Pueblo Grande. The site, administered by the Arizona Museum of Natural History, also contains a replica of a Hohokam ballcourt.

PAINTED ROCK PETROGLYPH SITE

» Hohokam Culture and Others

Painted Rock Petroglyph Site lies about a dozen miles (19 km) west of Gila Bend, an agricultural town along the Gila River that in turn lies about seventy-five miles (120 km) southwest of downtown Phoenix. Some of the petroglyphs likely date to the Hohokam period, while others are probably later, though in the same style as the Hohokam carvings. Many others predate the Hohokam altogether, belonging to the Archaic peoples of the desert.

Painted Rocks, as the site is informally known, is one of the largest concentrations of petroglyphs in the entire Southwest, including representations of animals, human figures, and abstract symbols. With the exception of the Three Rivers Mogollon Culture site (see page 52–53), it is also the most accessible of all the major petroglyph sites in the Southwest, with a paved road leading from Interstate 8 to the weathered mound of inscribed boulders.

Works of ancient rock art, such as these petroglyphs found at Painted Rock Petroglyph Site, Arizona, record the ways of animals, stars, and people over time and space. Numerous abstract images figure as well, the meanings of which have prompted much scholarly debate.

» Park of the Canals
   1710 North Horne Street
   Mesa, AZ 85203
   (480) 644-2351

» Mesa Grande Cultural Park
   1000 N. Date Street
   Mesa, AZ 85201
   (480) 644-3075

» Painted Rock
   Petroglyph Site
   Rocky Point Road
   Dateland, AZ 85333
   (623) 580-5500

Only the walls remain at Tusayan Pueblo, an ancient site at the Grand Canyon.

Below: This split twig figurine, perhaps representing a deer, was made between two thousand and four thousand years ago by a member of what archaeologists call the Archaic Culture. The figurine was found in a cave high along the walls of the Grand Canyon.

Right: An artist's depiction of Tusayan Pueblo commemorates its view of the San Francisco Peaks of northern Arizona.

Opposite: Petroglyphs such as these have outlived the centuries on the rock walls of Royal Arch Canyon, within Arizona's Grand Canyon National Park.

GRAND CANYON NATIONAL PARK
» Ancestral Pueblo Culture and Others

The archaeological record in the Grand Canyon, like the geological one, contains gaps and puzzles. More than four thousand years ago, the so-called Archaic people were living in caves and niches high up on its walls, where archaeologists have found their distinctive figurines made of split twigs. The Ancestral Pueblo people were building pithouses along the rim and in the inner canyon more than 1,500 years ago, and at the same time, a nonrelated people, the Cohonina, were also settling in the area. A small pithouse village located near the site of present Grand Canyon Village attests to their presence, but not much is known of these latter people, who lend their name to Arizona's Coconino County.

Nearly 1,500 Ancestral Pueblo sites have been identified to date within the boundar-ies of present-day Grand Canyon National Park. One that is open to visitation is Tusayan Pueblo, built about 1185 and located about twenty miles (32 km) east of Grand Canyon Village, not far from the Desert View Watchtower. The small U-shaped pueblo, with a kiva and storage rooms, was occupied for only about twenty years, perhaps by members of a single extended family. A small museum on the site contains remains from it and other excavations.

Tusayan is easily accessible, as are the Walhalla Ruins on the North Rim, overlooking the ancient farmlands of the Unkar Delta far below. Many other sites in the Grand Canyon are not so easily reached, however. A visit to Bright Angel Ruin, for example, requires a hike deep into the canyon, albeit on one of its most heavily traveled trails. The unmaintained Nankoweap Trail on the North Rim is considered among the most difficult in the Grand Canyon, but following it leads to a well-preserved ancient granary. Fortunately, the granary lies close to the Colorado River and is a frequent port of call for rafters traveling downstream. So is the Hilltop Ruin, which lies near the mouth of Cardenas Canyon and affords a fine 360-degree view of the canyon.

Some years ago, archaeologists surveyed about sixty sites along the Colorado River that were being eroded by water and wind. Between 2007 and 2009, they excavated nine of those sites, many about a thousand years old, and discovered, among other things, a kiva, a bison bone, and gaming pieces. The archaeologists also turned up evidence that the people there were growing cotton as well as squash, corn, and other crops in one of the most remarkable natural settings on Earth.

» Grand Canyon National Park
P.O. Box 129
Grand Canyon, AZ 86023
(928) 638-7888
www.nps.gov/grca

Above and left: Ancestral Puebloans built numerous dwellings and other structures, such as this row of granaries near Nankoweap Canyon, in recesses in the cliffs of the Grand Canyon. Well-preserved artifacts have been found within many of them, including ears of corn grown in fields along the river.

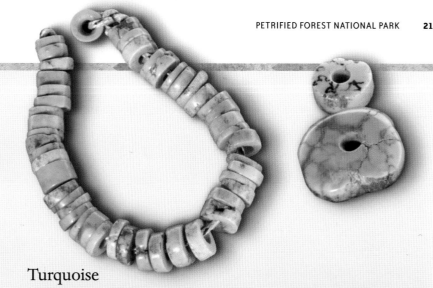

PETRIFIED FOREST NATIONAL PARK
» Ancestral Pueblo Culture and Others

Lying about a hundred miles (160 km) east of Flagstaff, Arizona, Petrified Forest is the only national park devoted to the Triassic period, which, some 225 million years ago, marked the rise of the great reptiles and ancestral birds collectively known as dinosaurs. The Triassic also saw the flourishing of giant coniferous trees the size of modern redwoods and even taller, which, buried in silt and volcanic ash, were eventually "petrified," their cells replaced by sand and minerals. Founded in 1906 as a national monument and upgraded to park status in 1962, Petrified Forest National Park preserves fossil remains of those creatures and those giant trees, the latter long since turned to

Above right: Sinagua jewelry from Tuzigoot National Monument. Below: In one interpretation of this ancient petroglyph, a waterbird uses its bill to spear an unfortunate frog, which has a strangely human form. The petroglyph is found near Puerco Pueblo at Petrified Forest National Park.

Turquoise

Turquoise, a hydrous phosphate of copper and aluminum, is a mineral prized wherever it is found in the world. That has certainly been true in the Southwest, where archaeologists have identified more than two hundred prehistoric mines that provided the materials for a rich tradition of turquoise jewelry.

When Pueblo Bonito, in Chaco Canyon (see pages 55–57), was first excavated in 1896, archaeologists found thousands on thousands of turquoise beads, as well as bits of mosaic inlay and figurines. Nearby Fajada Butte was the site of a turquoise workshop whose products have been found as far south as Mesoamerica. In the 1930s, when Emil Haury and Harold Gladwin excavated the Hohokam site of Snaketown, not far from Casa Grande Ruins National Monument, they found thousands of beads, inlaid shells and bones, mosaics, and other ornaments made of the alluring blue stone.

yellow, pink, purple, and green rock.

Often overlooked is the long human presence within the park. Archaeologists have identified several places within Petrified Forest associated with the Archaic tradition, dating back 8,000 years and more, including projectile points, scrapers, and hearths. Basketmaker people, forebears of the Ancestral Puebloans, built pithouses here and there. From a later era, Agate House, an eight-room pueblo occupied from about 1125 CE to 1225 CE, lies a short distance from the popular visitor destination called Long Logs. Some sites have given evidence, in the form of architectural and ceramic remains, of affinities to Chaco Canyon, while much of the pottery found in the park is of Mogollon origin, which indicates that the people here traded widely with their neighbors to the south and east as well.

If you enter Petrified Forest from the northern entrance along Interstate 40, as most travelers do, you will first come to a well-appointed visitor center with a restaurant and bookstore. From it, the road turns south, crosses the interstate highway, and traverses the Puerco River valley, slowly

climbing another low mesa. Here are the ruins of Puerco Pueblo, built sometime before 1000 by the Ancestral Pueblo people. It was then vacated after about a century before being reoccupied in about 1300 CE. At its height, Puerco had about a hundred rooms surrounding a central plaza and probably housed a population of two hundred people. Puerco Pueblo also boasts a solar marker, a petroglyph that interacts with sunlight and shadow to mark celestial events. At the summer solstice, park rangers offer interpretive programs that help us understand how those ancient inhabitants viewed the heavens.

Puerco Pueblo (above) is one of several Ancestral Pueblo sites within Petrified Forest. Those people, and the cultures who came before them, made use of petrified wood in many ways, including shaping it into arrowheads.

Opposite: The remnants of forests 225 million years old lie scattered on the surface at Petrified Forest National Park.

» Petrified Forest
National Park
1 Park Road, P.O. Box 2217
Petrified Forest, AZ 86028
(928) 524-6228
www.nps.gov/pefo/
index.htm

Above: Six major sites at the Ancestral Pueblo settlement of Homol'ovi, "the place of the little hills," date to between 1260 and 1290. A seventh was added after 1350. The sturdy walls and small rooms bespeak a collection of buildings that housed many hundreds of people at a time.

Opposite: White House Ruin, in Canyon de Chelly, is among the best-known Ancestral Pueblo sites. A cliffside trail leads to the pueblo, built around 1075.

» Homol'ovi State Park
  HCR 63, Box 5
  Winslow, AZ 86047
  (928) 289-4106
  www.pr.state.az.us/Parks/
  HORU/index.html

HOMOL'OVI STATE PARK
» *Ancestral Pueblo Culture and Others*

In the Hopi language, Homol'ovi means "place of the little hills," a name given to what Anglos call Winslow, Arizona. There, between 1260 and 1290, Ancestral Puebloans—whom the Hopi call Hisat'sinom, "long-ago people"—founded six pueblos, with a seventh added after 1350, adjacent to fertile fields along the Little Colorado River. Prior to the construction of the pueblos, the Homol'ovi area was occupied between 600 CE and 1225 CE by small groups who lived in pithouses. After a brief hiatus, migrants from the north built the large pueblos. The largest pueblo, Homol'ovi II, was founded after 1350 and contains more than 1,200 rooms, which held an estimated one thousand occupants at its peak around 1385. The site also includes three plazas and about forty kivas.

The Hopi people consider the settlers of Homol'ovi to be among their ancestors and the area to be an ancestral homeland. They also consider it a living place, for which reason the former name of the site, Homol'ovi Ruins State Park, was amended to its present form.

CANYON DE CHELLY
NATIONAL MONUMENT
» *Ancestral Pueblo Culture*

The Navajo word Tséyi', which Spanish explorers pronounced "Chelly" and Anglos "Shay," means "within the rock," a general term for canyon. Located in northeastern Arizona about two hundred miles (322 km) from Flagstaff, Canyon de Chelly is a place of towering red and white sandstone walls that enclose a maze of side canyons: Canyon de Chelly proper, as well as Canyon del Muerto and Monument Canyon and their tributaries, an area extending over 131 square miles (339 sq km).

Canyon de Chelly contains more than eight hundred known archaeological sites representing almost the entire range of Ancestral Pueblo house forms, from pithouses and surface pueblos to cliff dwellings. The best way to get a sense of the place is to follow two scenic routes, the thirty-six-mile (58 km)-long South Rim Drive, with seven overlooks, and the thirty-four-mile (55 km)-long North Rim Drive, with three overlooks. On South Rim Drive, White House Overlook, for example, offers both a view of the Ancestral Pueblo cliff dwelling of that name,

as well as access to it by way of a 2.5-mile (4 km)-long trail. White House is probably the best-known Ancestral Pueblo structure in Canyon de Chelly, and is certainly among the most visually striking in the whole Ancestral Pueblo world. Another must-see South Rim point is Spider Rock, about which the Navajo people—and doubtless their Ancestral Pueblo predecessors—have developed a fine body of stories and songs. The rock spire rises 750 feet (229 m) from the desert floor, an island of sandstone marooned by erosion over millions of years.

North Rim Drive, which mostly follows Canyon del Muerto, offers a view of Antelope House, located where a tributary called Black Rock Canyon enters it. There, long ago, an artist drew a series of paintings of running antelope, designs that were emulated by other artists of the time and that turn up in pottery and jewelry made today.

Some archaeologists believe that a number of sites in Canyon de Chelly were settled by immigrants from Chaco Canyon, Mesa Verde, and other Ancestral Pueblo centers, though these sites were not settled for long; the last, the village at Mummy Cave, was departed in about 1285. The structures are fascinating, and many are in good condition, but Canyon de Chelly is also very well known for its rock art, which archaeologists have carefully documented. Ancient knowledge of the night sky is abundantly commemorated here as well. What some believe are dozens of planetaria are painted on walls, ledges, and caves, recording the movement of the constellations and other celestial events.

Though administered as a national monument, Canyon de Chelly belongs to the Navajo Nation. Travelers are permitted to enter the canyon on foot with a Navajo guide, but it is much too big to explore that way. Travel by private vehicle also requires hiring a Navajo guide. A list of approved guides is available at the visitor center. Plan to spend at least a full day to see the principal sites, which are among the greatest archaeological treasures in the Southwest. Half- and full-day tours are also available, departing from the Sacred Canyon Lodge (www.sacredcanyonlodge.com) at the mouth of the canyon.

Above: The village at Mummy Cave, in Canyon de Chelly, was inhabited until about 1285.

Opposite: Spider Rock, a spire of sandstone, lies deep within Canyon de Chelly at the point where Monument Canyon joins it. The spire rises 750 feet (229 m) from the desert floor.

» Canyon de Chelly
National Monument
PO Box 588
Chinle, AZ 86503
(928) 674-5500
www.nps.gov/cach

After decades of exploration, Archaeologists are still making significant finds at Navajo National Monument, which includes Keet Seel. The long ladders could be pulled away for defensive purposes, making the cliffside dwelling even more secure. It was abandoned in the 13th century.

Below: A seed jar made in the Keet Seel polychrome style.

Opposite: Towering walls of sandstone dwarf the human settlements of Betatakin within Navajo National Monument.

» Navajo National
Monument
Shonto, AZ 86054
(928) 672-2700
www.nps.gov/nava

NAVAJO NATIONAL MONUMENT

» Ancestral Pueblo Culture

You can see them from a long way away, the magnificent cliff dwellings known as Betatakin and Keet Seel (respectively "ledge house" and "broken pottery," in Navajo), commanding a view of the broad Tsegi Canyon, located about 140 miles (225 km) northeast of Flagstaff.

Tsegi Canyon and its side canyons have been settled for thousands of years by people across a range of cultures; and like Canyon de Chelly, the structures here are of importance to the Navajo people who live in the region today. Both Betatakin and Keet Seel were built by people formerly called the Kayenta Anasazi, a distinct branch of the Ancestral Pueblo people who settled in the area of what is now northeastern Arizona and parts of southwestern Utah. People from other branches—notably Chacoans and Mesa Verdeans—lived among them in separate communities. Facing a dense aspen grove and reached by a five-mile (8 km)-long, challengingly steep walk, Betatakin is a multistoried pueblo of 135 rooms built beneath the overhanging wall of a huge wind cave that reaches five hundred feet in height. Construction of Keet Seel probably began in the 1240s, while Betatakin began about forty years later. The latter was occupied for just thirty or forty

years, an immense expenditure of effort that speaks to a need to migrate. Evidence of later Kayenta settlement in central and southern Arizona has been found, but no one is quite sure where the people went.

Keet Seel lies about eight miles (13 km) from the visitor center along a sometimes precipitous trail leading into a tributary of Tsegi Canyon. Richard Wetherill, who had earlier explored Mesa Verde, systematically explored the ruins, which contain more than 150 rooms and numerous kivas. Because of its sheltered location, it is among the best preserved of all Ancestral Pueblo ruins.

Getting to almost every part of Navajo National Monument requires planning, stamina, strength, and supplies of food and water. These sites lie a long way from modern settlements, and they're not for the faint of heart—though seeing them most definitely repays the effort.

Casa Malpais, a Mogollon site near the Little Colorado River, was built of volcanic rock in about 1260.

Below: Sunset Crater, near the San Francisco Mountains, is the heartland of the Sinagua Culture.

Opposite: Wupatki National Monument contains more than 2,700 archaeo-logical sites, including the namesake pueblo, whose name means "tall house" in Hopi.

CASA MALPAIS ARCHAEOLOGICAL PARK AND MUSEUM

» Mogollon Culture

Most Mogollon sites, such as the well-known Gila Cliff Dwellings (see pages 51–52), lie in what is now New Mexico. An outlier is the Casa Malpais, a Mogollon pueblo of about sixty rooms near Springer-ville, Arizona, not far from the New Mexico border at an elevation of about seven thousand feet (2,133 m). Located near the Little Colorado River, it was built of local volcanic rock atop a heavily fissured rock surface in about 1260 CE and occupied for only about a hundred years. An opening on the northern side of a round structure called the Solar Calendar is oriented to true north, and other openings appear to have been designed to observe the summer and winter solstices. Though a Mogollon site, the material remains found at Casa Malpais show plenty of Ancestral Pueblo influences. The museum there offers scheduled tours of the site, and it houses artifacts from excavations there and elsewhere in the area.

» Casa Malpais
Archaeological Park
and Museum
418 East Main Street
Springerville, AZ 85938
(928) 333–5375
www.casamalpais.org

WUPATKI NATIONAL MONUMENT

» Sinagua Culture

Sometime between 1064 and 1067, a small volcanic mountain to the east of the San Francisco Peaks erupted, creating what is now Sunset Crater. The sight must have been frightening to behold, but the ash fall had the positive effect of enriching a soil that was not particularly fertile before, giving the Sinagua the basis of a newly rich agriculture. Built on the edge of a low canyon,

Lomatki Ruin, in the foreground at sunrise, enjoys a panoramic view of the 12,633 feet (3,851 m) high San Francisco Peaks in the distance.

Below: A palette of dried paint recovered from the ruins at Wupatki National Monument.

» Wupatki National
   Monument
   6400 N. Hwy 89
   Flagstaff, AZ 86004
   (928) 679–2365
   www.nps.gov/wupa

Wupatki Pueblo, about thirty-five miles (56 km) northeast of Flagstaff, eventually came to include more than a hundred multistory rooms, as well as a ballcourt and a large central plaza.

The centerpiece of the national monument, which contains more than 2,700 archaeological sites, is the multistory Wupatki Ruin, which explains the name of the complex, meaning "tall house" in the Hopi language. The ruin contained about a hundred rooms, larger than most Sinagua structures, and it shows influences from the nearby Kayenta Ancestral Pueblo tradition as well as that of more distant Chaco Canyon. Its ballcourt suggests an influence from Hohokam settlements in the Verde Valley below the Mogollon Rim—or possibly even

the presence of Hohokam immigrants in the village. The whole settlement was built of red sandstone in the twelfth century. Unusually, it is situated near a blowhole, or wind cave, that emits cool air during the heat of the day, providing a kind of natural air-conditioning.

Near Wupatki, at the brow of a low hill, stands the Citadel Ruin, a surface pueblo containing about fifty rooms. The Citadel has only a single entrance, which suggests that its purpose may have been defensive, as does the fact that it offered line-of-sight communication with all the other pueblos in the vicinity, such as Nalakihu ("small house," in the Hopi language), which lies just below the citadel.

Wupatki had a number of surrounding pueblos, including Wukoki, Lomaki, and possibly even distant Elden Pueblo outside Flagstaff. It is important to the modern-day Hopi people, who consider it an ancestral place. Plan to take the better part of the day to see the key sites, which are scattered over an area of more than fifty-five square miles (142 sq km).

WALNUT CANYON NATIONAL MONUMENT
» *Sinagua Culture*

In about 1125, the Sinagua began to build a winding, difficult-to-access series of structures in recesses among the limestone walls of steep Walnut Canyon, located about ten miles (16 km) southeast of present-day Flagstaff. By the time they left the site some 125 years later, they had built more than eighty cliff dwellings. Most of them are small—perhaps a dozen feet in length, and half as many in width—suggesting occupancy by single families. The canyon walls lacked permanent water sources, requiring trips down dizzying paths into the canyon, where a perennial stream flowed and the people of Walnut Canyon kept their fields. The Sinagua residents of Walnut Canyon improved those trails over the years to make some of the grades less strenuous, but getting to the valley floor took work, and getting back up laden with earthenware jars of water took more effort still.

Even with its challenges, though, Walnut Canyon was an excellent place to live, for the Mogollon Rim country is rich in wildlife and plant life alike, affording plenty of access to food. Visitors today can follow a modern trail—a steep one of 240 steps—that leads to some of the cliff dwellings. The trail is less than a mile (1.6 km) round-trip, but even experienced hikers may find themselves huffing and puffing on the way back up.

Ancient Weaving

Agaves grow just about everywhere in the Southwest. Those plants provide edible seeds, fruit, and pulp. When their leaves are scraped away, they yield fiber—and the sharp end of the leaf even provides a needle—making agaves a widely used source of clothing.

The ancient peoples of the Southwest made use of many other materials for weaving. Archaeologist Harold Baldwin identified some of them as apocynum (a kind of hemp); cedar and juniper bark; human hair; and the fur or hair of dogs, bears, rabbits, and sheep. The ancient peoples of the Southwest were also fond of wearing feathers, especially those of exotic birds such as macaws.

Cotton was also extensively used, the only crop grown only for fiber. It has been found in Hohokam, Ancestral Pueblo, Mogollon, and Sinagua sites, beginning in about 700 CE. Archaeologist Emil Haury discovered a cache of cotton stored in a remote cave in the Pinaleño Mountains of southeastern Arizona that dated to about a thousand years before the present.

Above: Ancestral Pueblo people wore woven sandals such as this one, a rare artifact that is now preserved in the museum at Aztec Ruins National Monument, New Mexico.

Left: Sturdy walls enclose a row of dwellings under natural rock overhangs along the Island Trail at Walnut Canyon National Monument, Arizona.

» Walnut Canyon
National Monument
3 Walnut Canyon Road
Flagstaff, AZ 86004
(928) 526-3367
www.nps.gov/waca

PALATKI, HONANKI, AND V-BAR-V PETROGLYPH CULTURAL HERITAGE SITES

» *Sinagua Culture and Others*

Palatki, located about fifteen miles (24 km) from downtown Sedona, Arizona, is a pueblo consisting of two large structures built between 1130 and 1280. Their red fitted stones lend the pueblo its name, which means "red house" in the Hopi language. The pueblo's buildings probably housed five to seven related families, since pictographs interpreted as clan totems, signaling ownership, have been found in association with them. The nearby cliffs shelter numerous well-preserved pictographs and petroglyphs from the same era, though some of those images are much older, and some containing depictions of horses are obviously later. For reservations to visit Palatki, call (928) 282-3854.

Honanki lies about 2.5 miles (4 km) beyond Palatki along a rough dirt road that is sometimes impassable in inclement weather. It represents the remains of a sixty-room pueblo built at about the same time as Palatki, tucked against the side of a towering red-walled cliff. Both sites were vacated by the Sinagua around 1300, although the site was later used by the Yavapai on a seasonal basis.

The V-Bar-V Ranch Petroglyph Site, which lies about eight miles (13 km) southeast of Sedona and just a couple of crow-flight miles from Montezuma Well, contains some of the best-preserved examples of Sinagua petroglyphs in existence today. The Forest Service road leading to it is a little bumpy, and it takes a mile (1.6 km)-long round trip to walk to the site, but the place is remarkable and well worth taking time to visit.

» Coconino National Forest
Red Rock Ranger District
8375 State Route 179
Sedona, AZ 86351
(928) 203–2900
www.coconinonational
forest.us
www.sedonaredrock
trails.com

Right: Petroglyphs at the V-Bar-V site, where some of the best-preserved Sinagua rock art is to be found.

Below: Palatki, whose name means "red house" in Hopi, housed the members of several families over the decades between 1130, when construction was begun, and 1300, when the village was abandoned.

TUZIGOOT NATIONAL MONUMENT

» Sinagua Culture

Located about twenty-four miles (39 km) southwest of Sedona just outside the small town of Clarkdale, Tuzigoot National Monument stands at the crest of a small ridge above the sinuous Verde River. The river lends the 110-room pueblo its Apache name, meaning "crooked water." Completed in about 1125 CE, the two-story pueblo has only a few doorways; the residents had to come in and out by way of ladders. In about 1200, and again a century later, Sinagua builders expanded on the original pueblo, which came to contain eighty-seven ground-floor rooms surrounding a plaza. The site held about two hundred people comfortably. The pueblo was likely vacated by about 1425. Some archaeologists speculate that the people who once lived there moved to the high Colorado Plateau, briefly occupying the pueblo that is now preserved at Homol'ovi State Park.

Unlike many other Sinagua ruins, the interior of Tuzigoot is open to visitors. A self-guided loop trail takes in the whole of the site, with a short extension leading to an overlook above the river. The visitor center also contains a fine museum, among whose holdings are rare split-twig figurines and other materials found in the pueblo and sites in nearby Sycamore Canyon.

» Tuzigoot National Monument
PO Box 219, Camp Verde, AZ 86322
(928) 567–5276 www.nps.gov/tuzi

Tuzigoot National Monument, a pueblo completed in about 1125, commands a view of the Verde Valley and adjacent Tavasci Marsh. Its interior (below) was made of sturdy beams and courses of carefully laid stone. Left: Hohokam traders, or perhaps settlers, introduced this Hohokam carving to the site.

MONTEZUMA CASTLE NATIONAL MONUMENT
» *Sinagua Culture*

Montezuma Castle lies downstream of Montezuma Well on Beaver Creek, a tributary of the nearby Verde River. Both are easily accessible by paved roads that lead from Interstate 17, the main highway connecting Phoenix to Flagstaff and nearby Sedona. The well is a limestone sink that brings up more than 1.5 million gallons of water a day from deep in the earth. American newcomers who came to the area in the mid–nineteenth century bestowed the name "Montezuma" on the place because they imagined that the Aztecs had to have built the remarkable structure they called Montezuma Castle, though it was the southern Sinagua people who constructed the pueblo.

Montezuma Castle is a five-story cliff dwelling that stands a little more than a hundred feet above the floor of a cottonwood-lined canyon, where the people grew a variety of crops. Some archaeologists suggest that the T-shaped doors show the influence of Ancestral Pueblo great house architecture, while trade goods such as feathers and seashells found there prove that the people of Montezuma Castle participated fully in regional trade networks. Built around 1125 and occupied until about 1400, the "castle" contains about twenty rooms, most of them in remarkably good shape thanks to the natural protection of the limestone cliff. It was

Montezuma Castle is a five-story-tall Sinagua cliff dwelling built in about 1125. Below: Montezuma's Well, a nearby spring, assured a constant supply of fresh water, a rare boon in the desert.

one of the very first places put under the protection of the National Park Service and was declared a national monument by none other than President Theodore Roosevelt in 1906. Today it is one of the best-preserved cliff dwellings in America, with a visitor center that contains an excellent museum devoted to the Sinagua Culture.

At the foot of the cliff, a couple of hundred feet (60 m) away from Montezuma Castle proper, stand the largely disintegrated remains of a forty-five-room pueblo called Castle A, which is about the same age. Archaeologists speculate that most of the people of the area lived there except in times of emergency, when they withdrew to the higher fortress.

AGUA FRIA NATIONAL MONUMENT
» Sinagua Culture and Others

Designated as a national monument in 2000, Agua Fria contains a huge number of archaeological sites that represent the Hohokam and other prehistoric cultures—and, located roughly midway between Phoenix and the Mogollon Rim, it makes a natural meeting place for the two traditions. Archaeologists have deemed the people who lived there between 1250 and 1450 the "Perry Mesa tradition," after a site representing the distinct culture that the people there made of those Hohokam and other prehistoric traditions. Only about three thousand people lived in

this rugged country, but they left behind a couple of well-developed pueblos, including Pueblo la Plata, a settlement of about a hundred rooms. The Perry Mesa people left the area as late as 1500 CE, and not long after, the Apache and Yavapai people made it their own.

Interstate 17 passes through the vast monument, but most of the roads leading through it are rough and require a four-wheel-drive vehicle. Out on the land, archaeologists have catalogued about five hundred sites so far, but many others await discovery and analysis. Perry Mesa is jointly owned by the Bureau of Land Management and the National Forest Service, but only the BLM side is currently included within the Agua Fria National Monument.

Located only forty miles (64 km) from downtown Phoenix, the monument offers numerous hiking trails that lead to many of these sites. There are no facilities, so be sure to bring adequate supplies of food and water.

TONTO NATIONAL MONUMENT
» Salado Culture

On a cliff hundreds of feet above the Tonto Basin, about a hundred miles (160 km) east of downtown Phoenix, stands the Salado settlement best known to us today, Tonto National Monument. The Salado are arguably the least-studied prehistoric culture in the Southwest, having long been considered to be something of the poor cousins of the better-known Ancestral Pueblo or Hohokam peoples, but a visit to Tonto shows that the Salado were just as adept in building, farming, and creating lasting works of art.

The monument consists of two distinct areas. The Upper Cliff Dwelling consists of thirty-two ground floor rooms. Eight of them had a second story, and the entire structure was topped with a terrace. The only way to visit it at present is to sign on to a tour led by a park ranger, and it's a good idea to book this in advance of a visit. The Lower Cliff Dwelling, which lies at the end of a steep, winding one-mile trail from the visitor center, has sixteen ground-floor rooms, three of which had a second story. Again, a smooth terrace capped the structure, reached by ladders from the rooms

Left: A diorama depicts daily life within the Sinagua village at Montezuma Castle.

Pages 38–39: A view from the Upper Cliff Dwelling of Tonto National Monument. The Tonto Basin, which lies below Tonto National Monument, is now the site of the vast reservoir called Roosevelt Lake. In prehistoric times, it was a rich source of game and plant food for the Salado people who made their homes in the cliff dwellings here.

» Montezuma Castle
   National Monument
   PO Box 219
   Camp Verde, AZ 86322
   (928) 567–5276
   www.nps.gov/moca

» Agua Fria National
   Monument
   BLM Phoenix Field Office
   21605 North 7th Avenue
   Phoenix, AZ 85027
   (623) 580–5500
   www.blm.gov/az/st/en/
   prog/blm_special_areas/nat-
   mon/afria.html

below. Some of these rooms were residences, while others were work areas, granaries, and storage rooms. It was here that the Salado people wove textiles and made the intricate pottery for which they were famed, and which they traded throughout the Southwest.

The cliff dwellings of Tonto National Monument were vacated in about 1450. By this time, the population there numbered in the hundreds.

BESH-BA-GOWAH ARCHAEOLOGICAL PARK
» *Salado Culture*

Not far from the Salt River, which gives the Salado Culture its name, and also not far from the Gila River, stands Besh-Ba-Gowah Archaeological Park, a large village founded by the Hohokam in about 550 CE and later occupied by the Salado people. The numerous buildings there contained a total of about 145 ground-floor rooms, with about sixty second-story rooms, one of which has been restored and equipped with household goods that Salado people would have used, including agave textiles, sandals, and other clothing. The buildings faced out onto a large plaza that doubled as a cemetery from which about 150 graves have been excavated, some containing turquoise, obsidian, and other prized minerals.

A somewhat smaller village, Gila Pueblo, lies about two miles (3.2 km) from Besh-Ba-Gowah Archaeological Park. At around 1400, Gila Pueblo burned to the ground. Many remains were found, and some archaeologists believe the pueblo was attacked. The survivors moved away, leaving most of their possessions behind them.

The park also contains a fine museum and ethnobotanical garden that grows crops that the Salado would have known. In the Western Apache language, by the way, Besh Ba Gowah is the name for the mining city of Globe, meaning "place of metal."

Above: A Salado bowl showcasing an animal motif was found on the site of the Besh-Ba-Gowah Pueblo.

Left: A reconstructed interior room at Besh-Ba-Gowah contains household goods that the Salado people would have used in their daily lives.

Opposite: The Salado Culture ruin at Tonto National Monument was built into a cliff face about 1300. Reaching it today requires a one-mile walk on a steep but well-made trail that winds through a forest of saguaro cacti, characteristic plants of the Sonoran Desert.

» Tonto National Monument
  HC 02 Box 4602
  Roosevelt, AZ 85545
  (928) 467–2241
  www.nps.gov/tont/index.htm

» Besh-Ba-Gowah
  Archaeological Park
  1324 South Jesse Hayes Road
  Globe, AZ 85501
  (928) 425–0320
  www.globeaz.gov/visitors/
  besh-ba-gowah

COLORADO

MESA VERDE NATIONAL PARK

» Ancestral Pueblo Culture

One of several large Ancestral Pueblo communities, Mesa Verde encompasses more than five thousand archaeological sites—including six hundred separate cliff dwellings—spread out over more than fifty thousand acres (20,000 ha), and the Mesa Verde culture area extended well beyond the Park's limits into Utah, Arizona, and New Mexico.

Mesa Verde, whose name means "green table," rises 8,500 feet (2,590 m) tall, like a giant island from the floor of the nearby piñon-juniper forests in far southwestern Colorado, affording sweeping views of the rumpled yellow-sandstone territory below.

Ancestral Pueblo people first began to build permanent structures at Mesa Verde about 550 CE, locating their pithouses on the mesa at an elevation of about seven thousand feet (2,133 m). Around 750 CE they began building above ground. There were springs and drainages between the cliffs, but almost no water on the mesa top. The springs harbored great groves of piñon pine that afforded them abundant building materials. About 1300 CE, their descendants left the mesa. Archaeologists propose several reasons for their departure, including a long-term drought, as well as other events and circumstances.

Three hundred fifty years later, Spanish explorers placed the great mesa as a landmark on their maps but kept their distance. The Utes had been there for years and others had investigated the area, but it wasn't until rancher and trader Richard Wetherill

Above: A Mesa Verde–style vessel found at Aztec Ruins National Monument, New Mexico.

Left: Several structures and rock recesses in Mesa Verde National Park are adorned with petroglyphs and pictographs made by the region's peoples over hundreds, and perhaps even thousands, of years. These markings appear on the Petroglyph Point Trail.

Opposite: Cliff Palace, the centerpiece of Mesa Verde National Park, is the largest cliff dwelling in North America.

Above: An exposed kiva, or underground chamber, in Balcony House. Getting to Balcony House requires a climb up a thirty-foot-tall ladder.

Below: Square Tower House, visible from an overview on the Mesa Verde National Park loop drive, stands four stories tall.

Opposite: Ladders lead from a plaza floor into subsurface kivas at Spruce Tree House. The T-shaped doorway seen in the foreground was a hallmark of Ancestral Pueblo architecture.

» Mesa Verde National Park
PO Box 8
Mesa Verde, CO 81330-0008
(970) 529-4465
www.nps.gov/meve

poked around in the late 1880s that the great "city" begin to give up its secrets. Bits and pieces of its remains were soon scattered to the winds. For one thing, Wetherill and subsequent explorers shipped great quantities of pottery, arrowheads, and other goods to museums and private collections throughout the world, but attention came through many other means as well.

Over the centuries, the Ancestral Pueblo people built a vast conglomerate of pueblos, including plazas and kivas. Around 1200 CE, however, they began to transfer their residences and storerooms from the top of the mesa to overhangs along its sandstone alcoves. Some of the structures on Mesa Verde are dizzying to behold, as if hanging in space, and certainly getting to them called for agility and no fear of heights.

To reach those structures during construction, the builders first had to dig footholds and staircases into the sandstone, then haul wood and other building materials year after year. Most of the cliffside structures contain ten rooms or fewer, but some are comparatively vast: Cliff Palace, at the heart of Mesa Verde and one of the best-known structures built by the Ancestral Puebloans, contains more than twenty kivas

and more than 150 rooms. Long House, on Wetherill Mesa, is about the same size, and it is just as impressive. Square Tower House is another great structure. Even the smaller structures, such as the forty-room Balcony House, were built with consummate care, and they are worth examining up close—though to get to Balcony House involves climbing up a thirty-foot-tall ladder, which calls for an adventurous spirit.

Cliff Palace is open to visitors April through November. The 130-room Spruce Tree House, which lies just below the museum, is open year-round. Some structures are closed because of structural issues, and some cliff dwellings can be visited only on tours guided by park rangers. Some of the most interesting, such as Oak Tree House and Spring House, are accessible by way of guided backcountry hikes, for which tickets, if the sites are currently open, are available at www.recreation.gov. The park also contains an excellent archaeological museum devoted to interpretation of the site, with superb dioramas made by Civilian Conservation Corps artists in the 1930s. Mesa Verde is a place of cold winters and tempestuous summer storms, so visitors should be prepared for dramatic weather.

Archaeoastronomy

The prehistoric peoples of the Southwest had a sophisticated knowledge of astronomy. High up Fajada Butte in Chaco Canyon (see pages 55–57), for example, some earlier astronomer laboriously carved grooves into the rock to mark the lunar standstill cycle, which occurs every 18.6 years. Many other markers in Chaco Canyon pinpoint solstices and other celestial events.

Throughout the Southwest, ancient observatories at places such as Casa Grande, Mesa Verde, Casa Malpais, and Wupatki mark the solstices and equinoxes. The ancient Greeks performed their tragic plays to coincide with such celestial events; perhaps the Hohokam, Mogollon, Ancestral Puebloans, and other ancient inhabitants of the Southwest had a similarly well-developed body of ceremony, observing the times when the rain gods traveled, animals moved, and the people were meant to dance and plant crops.

The Ancestral Puebloans vacated the greater Mesa Verde region in about 1300 CE, traveling in all directions; their descendants may be found among the Hopi people and all nineteen of New Mexico's Rio Grande pueblos as well as one in Texas.

CROW CANYON ARCHAEOLOGICAL CENTER
» *Ancestral Pueblo Culture*

Much of what we know about the Ancestral Pueblo people in the Mesa Verde area comes to us through research conducted at the Crow Canyon Archaeological Center, near Cortez. At the heart of its 170-acre (69 ha) campus is the Gates Building, which stands between two learning centers, one devoted to pithouses and the other to pueblos.

One important research program conducted by Crow Canyon took place at nearby Sand Canyon Pueblo, an ancient village that was occupied from 1250 to about 1280, only slightly longer than a generation. Sand Canyon contained some 420 rooms, ninety kivas, and fourteen towers, as well as an enclosed plaza, a formally constructed D-shaped building that probably served as an astronomical observatory, and a great kiva—all told, making Sand Canyon Pueblo three times as large as Mesa Verde's Cliff Palace. Crow Canyon conducted excavations at Sand Canyon Pueblo intermittently from 1984 until 1993. Only a small portion of the site was excavated, to preserve materials for future excavations. Artifacts from the excavations are housed at the Anasazi Heritage Center.

The Crow Canyon Archaeological Center campus is open to visitors weekdays from April 1 through October 31.

Above: An often overlooked upper structure at Spruce Tree House, one of hundreds of structures within Mesa Verde National Park, yields a view of Spruce Canyon below and the star-filled sky above.

» Crow Canyon Archaeological Center
   23390 Road K, Cortez, CO 81321–9408
   (970) 565–8975 www.crowcanyon.org

Painted Hand Pueblo contains the ruins of a stone tower that offers expansive views of Sleeping Ute Mountain and other landmarks.

Middle: A turquoise-inlaid shell on view at the Anasazi Heritage Center, a museum in Dolores, Colorado, devoted to Native cultures of the Four Corners region.

Below: Saddlehorn Pueblo takes its name from the distinctive rock formation above it.

CANYONS OF THE ANCIENTS NATIONAL MONUMENT

» Ancestral Pueblo Culture and Others

Headquartered in Dolores, Colorado, within easy sight of Mesa Verde, Canyons of the Ancients National Monument contains more than six thousand archaeological sites, many of them representing the entire spectrum of Ancestral Pueblo history. Saddlehorn Hamlet, for example, lies beneath an oddly shaped sandstone column that gives it its name, with lower rooms used for sleeping and storage and upper rooms for defensive purposes. Painted Hand Pueblo, named for a nearby pictograph, contains the remains of a once-tall stone tower perched atop a large boulder; it yields superb views extending for miles toward Sleeping Ute Mountain, a local landmark. Castle Rock Pueblo is about the same age as nearby Mesa Verde, and it was made up of some forty rooms, nine towers, and sixteen kivas. Some structures are being allowed to return slowly to the earth, in keeping with the view that this is the proper way of nature.

The monument's centerpiece is the Anasazi Heritage Center, a museum that also contains two twelfth-century archaeological sites. One is the twenty-two-room Escalante Pueblo, which serves as an interpretive site. The structure was completed in about 1130 CE. The other is the Dominguez Ruin, which, at only four rooms, probably housed a single family.

Lowry Pueblo National Historic Landmark is the only developed recreation area within the monument. With its stabilized walls and numerous rooms and kivas, it is also among its best-preserved sites. Sand Canyon, west of Cortez on the road toward Hovenweep National Monument (see pages 69–70), contains numerous Ancestral Pueblo sites and is a popular destination for hiking, horseback riding, and mountain biking. Check at the Canyons of the Ancients visitor center for a detailed map of trails and features.

» Canyons of the Ancients and Anasazi Heritage Center
27501 Highway 184
Dolores, CO 81323
(970) 882–5600
www.blm.gov/co/st/en/fo/ahc.html

The Eagle's Nest cliff dwelling hangs
as if suspended in air within a rock
alcove at Ute Mountain Tribal Park.

» Ute Mountain Tribal Park
P.O. Box 109
Towaoc, CO 81334
(970) 749–1452
www.utemountaintribalpark.
info/

UTE MOUNTAIN TRIBAL PARK
» *Ancestral Pueblo Culture and Others*

Ute Mountain Tribal Park, also located near
Cortez, contains thousands of archaeological sites spread out over 125,000 acres
(50,500 ha) of rugged high-desert country
along twenty-five miles (40 km) of the
Mancos River. Most of those sites, including several rich petroglyph galleries, are
contemporaneous with their more famous
cousins at Mesa Verde. Unlike the structures at Mesa Verde, however, those at Ute
Mountain Tribal Park have been left at their
original sites. Getting to those sites requires
a permit. It involves traveling for forty-two
miles (68 km) along dirt roads, most in
reasonably good condition but still spine-
rattling, and then hiking up steep trails and
climbing tall ladders.

One such site is the Eagle's Nest Cliff
Dwelling, which earns its name because of
golden eagles nesting in the cliff dwelling.
Reaching it requires climbing a forty-foot
(12 m) ladder that, though perfectly sturdy,
still involves a certain amount of faith. It's
a wonderful experience, but a challenging
one, too.

One of thousands of ancient petroglyphs within
Ute Mountain Tribal Park, this one likely depicting
humans, birds, and deer.

CHIMNEY ROCK NATIONAL MONUMENT

» Ancestral Pueblo Culture

Located in the San Juan Mountains between Durango and Pagosa Springs, Chimney Rock is one of the country's newest national monuments. It encompasses hundreds of sites and an area of more than 4,700 acres (1,900 ha), but its highlight is the twin-spired rock that gives the place its name. Below those spires stood a two-story pueblo (Great House) of fitted stone. At more than ninety miles (145 km) from Chaco Canyon (see pages 55–57) and about half that distance from Aztec Ruins (see page 58), Chimney Rock Pueblo was the farthest north and east that the Ancestral Pueblo people are known to have settled.

A pair of kivas, completed in about 1090, mark celestial events such as solstices and equinoxes. More important still, the overall layout of the site suggests that Chimney Rock marked the major lunar standstill (see page 46), with the Great House Pueblo itself situated to take in a full view of this rare event. Indeed, when the pueblo was refurbished in 1093 CE, the moon was rising above the site and between those great

rocks. This has led some archaeologists to believe that Chimney Rock was an important observatory and ritual center.

Guided and self-guided tours can be arranged in advance or at the visitor center. Following the payment of an entrance fee (see the website for details), a tour guide leads guests to the high mesa in their own vehicles. From there visitors can follow an easy paved trail to the Great Kiva or scramble up a steep, unimproved trail to the Great House Pueblo, which stands at an elevation of 7,600 feet (2,316 m). Several other archaeological sites lie between the parking area and the Great House Pueblo.

Chimney Rock, twin spires in the San Juan Mountains of southwestern Colorado, marks the northernmost reach of the Ancestral Pueblo world and the site of the lunar standstill. Below: One of the two kivas within the complex sits high on the ridgetop at Chimney Rock's Great House Pueblo.

» Chimney Rock
  National Monument
  P.O. Box 1662
  Pagosa Springs, CO 81147
  (970) 883–5359
  www.chimneyrockco.org

NEW MEXICO

BLACKWATER DRAW CLOVIS SITE

» *Clovis Culture*

Blackwater Draw is a usually dry wash, some eighty-five miles (137 km) long, that passes by Portales, New Mexico. There lies one of the earliest Clovis sites known to us. Certainly it is among the most important, for early excavations discovered evidence of human occupation, along with the remains of a Columbian mammoth, bison, camel, dire wolf, horse, and smilodon (sabertooth cat). The site has been excavated at several points over the last eight decades, providing some of the first evidence of mammoth hunting by groups of Clovis Culture hunters, and, just as important, the site contained a stratified record of Clovis, Folsom, Late Paleoindian, and Archaic Culture use of the site. It is exceedingly rare to have such a complete record of human occupation through time at one place on the landscape, so Blackwater Draw is a true treasure. The discoveries from this site are housed and displayed at the Blackwater Draw Museum on the campus of Eastern New Mexico University. The Blackwater Draw Clovis site is open to visitors, and it was recently designated a National Historic Landmark.

GILA CLIFF DWELLINGS NATIONAL MONUMENT

» *Mogollon Culture*

Located in southwestern New Mexico and built in the late thirteenth century, the Gila Cliff Dwellings refers to a large Mogollon village that, unusually, contained not only the cliff structures that give the site its name, but incorporated earlier habitation modes such as pithouses, pueblos, and caves simultaneously.

Getting to the Cliff Dwellings involves driving a winding road that climbs tall mountains and drops into low valleys; in many spots, the speed limit is only fifteen miles (24 km) an hour, and it takes about two hours to get to the visitor center from Silver City, the nearest town. After following the West Fork of the Gila River and entering the canyon that lies a little more than a mile from the visitor's center, you will walk up a well-signed path to the dwellings. From below, you will see seven caves, six occupied in ancient times. The smallest of them was likely occupied by a single family, while the others probably housed members of different families, possibly related by clan, probably ten or fifteen families in all. Archaeologists have identified forty-six separate rooms. Along with dwellings, the caves contain storerooms that, in good years, would have contained baskets and round-bottomed urns full of grain.

The Gila Cliff Dwellings lie close to perennial water and scenic views that can be attained along the path of several hiking trails that terminate at the visitors center. On the ridge on which they are built, water and crystallized salts broke the conglomerate rock and form a cozy natural shelter—or, more accurately, series of shelters—located a couple of hundred feet above a rocky canyon lined with ponderosa pine, walnut, oak, fir, and piñon trees and abundant agaves, all of which provided food, medicine, fibers for baskets and clothing, fuel, and the materials with which to build

Above: A graceful vessel, housed at the Luna Mimbres Museum in Deming, New Mexico, depicts a bird—perhaps a white-winged dove—in flight.

Opposite: Gila Cliff Dwellings National Monument, in southwestern New Mexico, lies at the heart of the ancient Mogollon world.

» Blackwater Draw
Eastern New Mexico
University
1500 South Avenue K
Portales, NM 88130
(575) 562–1011
www.enmu.edu/services/
museums/blackwater-draw

A T-shaped doorway at Gila Cliff Dwellings National Monument reflects cultural influences from Ancestral Pueblo peoples to the north. The Mogollon people traded with the Hohokam to the west and other Native groups to the south and east as well.

Right: A Mimbres pot, prized by collectors and students of Native American art resides at the Luna Mimbres Museum in Deming, New Mexico.

» Gila Cliff Dwellings
   National Monument
   HC 68 Box 100
   Silver City, NM 88061
   (575) 536-9461
   www.nps.gov/gicl

sturdy dwellings for the farmers who made their homes here.

Of note in the construction of the Gila Cliff Dwellings are the T-shaped doorways, which figure in Ancestral Pueblo sites such as Chaco Canyon (see pages 55–57). This has caused some scholars to argue that refugees from Chaco settled the area, though the thesis is controversial. One of those doorways has been precisely dated through dendrochronology (see page 59) to 1276 CE, the very beginnings of this settlement. The corncobs scattered on the floor, within reach of grinding implements called manos and metates, are more than seven hundred years old, contemporaneous with the construction of several of the buildings here.

Thanks to the abundance of those cobs, one might suppose that the people who lived in the Gila Cliff Dwellings lived principally on corn. Corn was an important food crop, to be sure, but other foods were prominent, not least wild game, which may have provided as much as half of the diet. The people of the highlands grew domesticated crops, hunted, and gathered wild foods

from the surrounding forest, much as the Apache peoples who came after them did.

At its height, archaeologists estimate, the Mimbres Mogollon Culture probably numbered no more than six thousand people. Only a few hundred, if that many, ever lived at the Gila Cliff Dwellings, and even they stayed only for a bit longer than a generation.

THREE RIVERS PETROGLYPH SITE
» *Mogollon Culture*

Located within sight of the dunes that give their name to White Sands National Monument, the Three Rivers Petroglyph Site lies at some distance from the Mogollon heartland. Yet it is unmistakably Mogollon, the work of people called the Jornada Mogollon, who over a period of five hundred years carved more than 21,000 depictions of birds, animals, fish, reptiles, plants, insects, and humans, as well as geometrical and abstract figures, into the boulders lying atop a rolling volcanic ridge north of the present-day town of Tularosa, New Mexico. The site contains the ruin of a small pueblo dating only to the end of the active presence of the Mogollon there, suggesting that in earlier years people traveled from afar to leave their marks on the oxidized rocks. At more than fifty acres (20 ha) in extent, Three Rivers is one of the largest, and certainly most accessible, petroglyph sites in the entire Southwest.

» U.S. Bureau of Land Management
   1800 Marquess Street, Las Cruces, NM 88005
   (575) 525–4300 www.blm.gov/nm/threerivers

Below: The Three Rivers Petroglyph Site, easily accessible to visitors, is a treasure house of rock art created by the ancient Mogollon people over several centuries.

The Ancient Southwestern Diet

The earliest people in the Southwest were hunters and gatherers. More properly, they were gatherers and hunters, for while game was not always available, food plants usually were, whether greens, roots, nuts, or seeds. Historians estimate that at the time the Spanish conquistadors arrived at the present borderlands of the United States and Mexico, the Native peoples of the region were making use of as many as 2,500 different kinds of plants for food, fiber, and medicine.

Maize came early to the Southwest from the Valley of Mexico, where it had been grown for thousands of years. Archaeologists have not identified just which culture received it first—and it may have arrived in several places in the region at about the same time. Squash, beans, and peppers followed corn and were widely grown.

Excavations at a Mogollon site called Bat Cave, on the southern end of the Plains of San Agustin in central New Mexico, show that the people had a broad variety of foods from which to draw: rabbits, badgers, raccoons, coyotes, red foxes, mountain lions, wood rats, mule deer, bison, turkeys, great horned owls, hawks, and ducks, along with corn, beans, squash, amaranth greens, and wild berries. It was a feast that many Europeans of the same era might have envied.

CHACO CULTURE
NATIONAL HISTORICAL PARK
» *Ancestral Pueblo Culture*

Chaco Canyon is the preeminent city of the ancient Southwest, occupied for hundreds of years and providing a home for thousands of people. Like the world's great cities today, it drew resources in from hundreds of miles away, It must have been a splendidly impressive place to see, with its dozens of tall buildings and towers. Even in ruins, it is spectacular, a must-visit destination that requires some effort to reach but is worth every bit of it.

Nowhere in the ancient Southwest were buildings so large and so opulent, neatly whitewashed and painted. A single three-story building in Pueblo Pintado, a great house about three miles (5 km) east of the head of Chaco Canyon, had 140 rooms—and that was among the area's smaller structures, surrounded by yet smaller buildings occupied by farmers who worked the fields along Chaco Wash. Conversely, Casa Rinconada, directly across from the tall mesa that commands the view above Chaco Canyon, was among the very largest kivas ever built in the Southwest, an amphitheater large enough to hold scores of people.

Pueblo Bonito, at the foot of a stairway down from that mesa, lies at the heart of what archaeologist Stephen Lekson has called "Downtown Chaco." The D-shaped structure, containing at least 650 rooms, is the largest great house in Chaco Canyon. We know from tree ring dating (see page 59) that it was planned and built over a three-century period, from about 850 to 1150, perhaps by artisans and priests. The house is oriented to the cardinal directions, features of the landscape, and avenues alike. A portion of Pueblo Bonito lies beneath a huge rockfall that calved off the mesa after a rainstorm in 1941, sending some five million pounds (2.3 million kg) of rock from what is appropriately called Threatening Rock pouring onto the pueblo below. That disaster was a long time in coming—and we know that the Chacoan builders foresaw it, because they propped up logs and stones against the rock face to keep it from crushing them. Even so, they were not deterred from locating the great stone house where they did.

Opposite: Pueblo Bonito is the largest of the great houses within Chaco Canyon National Historical Park. It was occupied for about four centuries. Note the blend of straight and curved walls, which enclosed an area of more than two acres and at least 650 rooms. The north-south wall, in near-perfect alignment, divides the pueblo into distinct halves.

Below: Casa Rinconada was one of the largest kivas ever built in the ancient Southwest, capable of holding more than a hundred people.

A doorway in Pueblo Bonito is in the classic T shape favored by Ancestral Pueblo builders.

» Chaco Culture
National Historical Park
P.O. Box 220
Nageezi, NM 87037–0220
(505) 786-7014
www.nps.gov/chcu

What surprises many modern visitors to Chaco Canyon is its intricate, precise stonework, laid out in elaborate, well-thought-through patterns. We admire the stone walls of Chaco today, but the people who lived there would not have seen them: instead, the stones were covered with plaster that protected the interior core from the elements. It took hundreds of masons, stonecutters, and architects twenty years to finish even some of the less complex structures, quarrying millions of stones from the mesa to build great houses such as Hungo Pavi and Pueblo Alto.

Some buildings in Chaco Canyon had ceilings that weighed as much as ninety tons. To provide the structural beams to support them, Chacoans felled more than a quarter of a million trees in the Chuska Mountains and other forested highlands more than fifty miles (80 km) away. How those trees were transported to Chaco remains a source of mystery, but we do know that the Ancestral Pueblo people had no pack animals, so getting the timber must have involved unfathomably difficult labor on the part of people.

Here and there stood earthen mounds with sloped sides, looking something like flat-topped pyramids. Everywhere, from the solstice marker atop Fajada Butte to the straight, level walls of Pueblo del Arroyo to the tower kivas of Chetro Ketl, every structure in Chaco Canyon served purposes that could be considered both practical and symbolic.

At the height of Chacoan civilization, in the 1000s, a dozen stone "apartment complexes" fanned out along a ten-mile (16 km) boulevard leading to and from Downtown Chaco, some of them four stories high and containing more than five hundred rooms. For all the habitable space those places afforded, archaeologists are divided on whether Chaco had much of a permanent population: some believe that the city was mostly given over to ceremonial uses, while others conjecture that it was a working urban center with a population numbering six thousand or more.

Beyond those complexes, from Chaco Canyon communities extended out for miles, joined by what some archaeologists have determined are roads, many with stone curbs. More than 150 communities have been identified outside the canyon that were part of the Chacoan World. Some of these settlements were colonies built by Chacoan migrants; others were well-established communities whose local leaders desired connection to the Chacoan economic and ritual world.

What is certain is that trade goods came in by way of the extensive road systems: copper bells and tropical birds from Mexico, ceramics from Utah, turquoise and other precious stones from throughout the Southwest—and from everywhere, too, abundant stores of corn, which reinforces the idea that other Ancestral Pueblo communities paid tribute to the rulers of the great city.

Was Chaco Canyon primarily religious, a collection of religious structures and sites of pilgrimage? Was it a political center? Was it a commercial hub where people gathered to trade? It may or may not have been all or any of these things. Perhaps more conjectural is the thought that the buildings and roads of Chaco Canyon collectively made up a great astronomical observatory, the keyholes and walls lining up with celestial events that played out over the millions of miles.

Like every other place in the ancient Southwest, even Chaco was vacated in time, left for us to behold now as one of the most spectacular archaeological sites in North America. It is a sobering thought that the makers of Chaco, over their lifetimes, saw only bits and pieces of their accomplishments, for it took generations to build the great city at a time when the Ancestral Pueblo people lived, on average, for no more than forty years.

There are two principal ways to get into Chaco Canyon, both washboard dirt roads. (A third entrance was recently closed, permanently as of this writing.) The easier route is from Highway 550 to the north; the southern route, from Highway 57, is not recommended for RV travel. The northern approach affords a view of the canyon that gradually unfolds as you turn off the road to the visitor center, which contains a not-to-be-missed museum and offers specialized guides focusing on different structures within the park.

Top: Pueblo del Arroyo, one of the "apartment complexes" within Chaco Canyon, lies along an avenue that, with other roads, radiates outward from the city center. Bottom: Located to the northwest of downtown Chaco Canyon, Peñasco Blanco is an unexcavated great house. On the trail leading to it, the Supernova Pictograph Site is believed to depict the 1054 celestial event that resulted in the formation of the Crab Nebula, an event commemorated by the ancient astronomers of Chaco.

Numerous hiking trails wind through the canyon. Be sure to stay on marked paths. If you have the time and energy, walk the trail that leads you atop the sandstone mesa, where ancient visitors would have been dazzled by the sight of the largest, most resplendent city they had ever seen.

Above: The great kiva at Aztec Ruins National Monument is the only one of its kind to have been completely restored. The principal restoration work took place in the 1930s.

Right: One of a dozen kivas at West Ruin. The 400-room pueblo was completed in the 1130s.

» Aztec Ruins
  National Monument
  84 Road 2900
  Aztec, NM 87410
  (505) 334-6174
  www.nps.gov/azru

» Salmon Ruins Museum,
  Library, and Research Center
  6131 Highway 64
  Bloomfield, NM 87413
  (505) 632-2013
  www.salmonruins.com

AZTEC RUINS NATIONAL MONUMENT
» *Ancestral Pueblo Culture*
Aztec Ruins is an outlier of Chaco Canyon, located fifty-five miles (88 km) north of Chaco, roughly midway between where the San Juan River and Animas River meet and what is now the New Mexico–Colorado state line. It was built in the twelfth century CE, mostly between 1110 and 1120, just above a fertile floodplain. The large, excavated West Ruin contained some four hundred multistory rooms and twelve kivas, along with a great kiva that is one of the largest outside Chaco proper. That great kiva is the only one in the Southwest to have been completely reconstructed, and it's worth a visit simply to have a look at the thoroughly impressive structure.

Aztec Ruins also boasted the third largest of all the Chacoan great houses, and several outlying structures and pueblos completed a sizable community. The visitor center contains finds from excavations here, but, like the artifacts at Chaco Canyon, most of them were taken to collections elsewhere, including the American Museum of Natural History in New York and the Smithsonian Institution in Washington, D.C.

Aztec Ruins outlasted Chaco by about a century, and refugees from Chaco and Mesa Verde may have joined the population there after those great communities fell. Then Aztec Ruins, too, was vacated in about 1275 CE.

SALMON RUINS
» *Ancestral Pueblo Culture*
Salmon Ruins is another Chacoan outlier, located about forty-five miles (72 km) north of Chaco Canyon on the San Juan River. It contained a three-story great house built between 1090 and 1116 and numbering about 300 rooms. The great kiva in the plaza was destroyed by a flood of the nearby river in the 1100s. Chacoans probably vacated the pueblo at about 1125, when other Ancestral

Puebloans from nearby areas occupied the site, staying there until about 1280.

The Salmon Ruins site is administered by the San Juan County Museum Association and is not a member of the National Parks system. It is open to visitors year-round for a modest entrance fee.

EL MORRO NATIONAL MONUMENT
» *Ancestral Pueblo Culture and Others*

Also called Inscription Rock, El Morro ("the hill" or "the headland" in Spanish) is a low sandstone mesa, clad with pine and juniper trees, that rises two hundred feet (60 m) above the desert about fifteen miles (24 km) from Ramah, New Mexico. Nearby valleys show evidence of earlier settlement, with pithouses dating to about 400 CE, but El Morro seems not to have been permanently settled until much later. Atop the mesa stand the ruins of two Ancestral Pueblo villages, Atsinna Pueblo, numbering some 355 rooms, and the smaller North Ruin,

The natural pool at El Morro National Monument is a welcome sight in a dry land.

also called North Atsinna. Both were built in the late 1200s and abandoned after about a hundred years; scholars believe that the last inhabitants moved to Zuni and Acoma pueblos, and the Zuni themselves consider Atsinna Pueblo to be part of their traditional homelands.

Tree Rings and Archaeology

In a drawer in the Laboratory of Tree Ring Research at the University of Arizona lie several chunks of wood, fine-grained and beautifully layered, that are five thousand years old, taken from a bristlecone pine that once grew atop a mountain in eastern Nevada.

We know precisely the age of old Prometheus, the name modern scientists at the lab gave that tree, because its core accumulated rings of annual growth. Another University of Arizona scientist, A. E. Douglass, had the insight, nearly a century ago, that we can date not just trees but also prehistoric ruins by establishing "ring chronologies" taken from wood samples from various archaeological sites. By 1937, Douglass had established such chronologies for a two-thousand-year period for ponderosa pines, Douglas firs, piñons, and junipers in the Southwest. He used this chronology to determine that two Ancestral Pueblo sites, Aztec Ruins and Pueblo Bonito, were made of timbers from the same area, but that Aztec was built some fifty years after Pueblo Bonito.

Above: Balcony House, in Mesa Verde National Park, showcases large beams of the sort used to date structures like it precisely with the methods of dendrochronology.

Below: An intaglio of a mountain lion inscribes a boulder at Petroglyph National Monument.

Right: An anthropomorphic figure in Rinconada Canyon, Petroglyph National Monument.

» El Morro National Monument
Ramah, NM 87321
(505) 783–4226
www.nps.gov/elmo

» Petroglyph National
Monument
6001 Unser Boulevard NW
Albuquerque, NM 87120
(505) 899-0205
www.nps.gov/petr

A two-mile (3.2 km)-long hiking trail winds from the Visitor Center up the bluff to the ruins—but that trail, though steep, is more comfortable than the cliff-face hand-holds that the ancients made to travel to the valley floor. Only portions of the mesa-top structures have been completely excavated and analyzed, including sixteen rooms and two large kivas belonging to Atsinna Pueb-lo. Interpretive signage there orients visitors to the site and the larger landscape.

Below the mesa, near a pool of water—a rarity in the desert—and under countless cliff swallow nests, can be found more than two thousand inscriptions, from thousand-year-old Native petroglyphs to nineteenth-century American graffiti. The best-known of these inscriptions was made by the Spanish conquistador Juan de Oñate, who camped at El Morro and inscribed it with the legend *"Paso por aqui el adelantado Don*

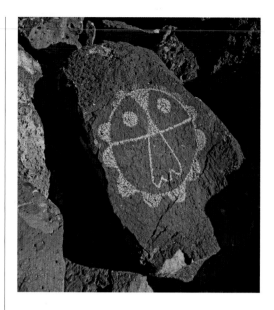

Ju[an] de Onate del descubrimyento de la mar del sur a 16 de Abril de 1605" ("Governor Don Juan de Oñate passed by here on the voyage of discovery of the Sea of the South"—that is, the Pacific Ocean, though Oñate actually found the Gulf of California—"on April 16, 1605"). Earlier, El Morro was a port of call for the Coronado Expedition of 1540–1542.

PETROGLYPH NATIONAL MONUMENT
» *Ancestral Pueblo Culture and Others*
Petroglyph National Monument hugs the lava escarpment known as West Mesa for seventeen miles (27 km) just west of downtown Albuquerque, taking in Rincon-ada Canyon, Mesa Prieta, Piedras Marcadas Canyon, and Boca Negra Canyon. Within its boundaries have been found more than 23,000 petroglyphs. Because of this rich-ness, Petroglyph National Monument is of inestimable importance to students of Southwestern prehistory. It is also of great importance to the modern Pueblo peoples.

Petroglyph National Monument contains numerous hiking trails of varying degrees of difficulty. Not all of the petroglyphs within it have been described and cata-logued. To complete that inventory will occupy scholars for years. Theirs is a race against time, not only because of the natu-ral forces of aging and erosion but also be-cause in many places the rock art has been threatened by vandalism and encroaching development.

CORONADO HISTORIC SITE

» *Ancestral Pueblo Culture and Others*

When Francisco Vásquez de Coronado traveled north along the Rio Grande, he did so with some four hundred Spanish soldiers and more than two thousand native allies. It was a terrible trip, but Coronado at least had the good fortune to see native settlements as they were before the arrival of European missionaries and administrators. One of the most impressive of them was Kuaua Pueblo, which now lies on the northern edge of metropolitan Albuquerque and has been designated the Coronado Historic Site (previously known as the Coronado State Monument).

Ancestral Pueblo people built Kuaua Pueblo in about 1325 CE, abandoning it shortly after Coronado visited in 1540, when a local war broke out. The site is well known for murals, recovered from a kiva, that were made before the European arrival. A visitor center, designed by the noted Southwestern architect John Gaw Meem, preserves these original murals. Replicas, drawn by renowned fresco painter Ma-Pe-Wi, can be seen inside the kiva proper

(though, please note, photography is not permitted there). Among the attractions at this New Mexico Historic Site is a small field house built of packed mud balls and an interpretive trail, which offers spectacular views of the Rio Grande Bosque and nearby Sandia Mountains.

BANDELIER NATIONAL MONUMENT

» *Ancestral Pueblo Culture and Others*

Adolph Bandelier (1840–1914), a Swiss immigrant who became an anthropologist after having been a successful businessman, came to the site of the monument that bears his name in 1880. He was struck by the majesty of its crumbling cliffs and the verdant beauty of the gallery forest lying alongside the neighboring Rio Grande between Santa Fe and Los Alamos, but what caught his attention were the abundant ruins, which seemed to lie everywhere.

Top: From their rooftops, reached by ladder, the residents of Kuaua Pueblo enjoyed a sweeping view of the Sandia Mountains and other Albuquerque-area landmarks.
Right: A bracelet made from the shell of a saltwater clam.

» Coronado Historic Site
485 Kuaua Road
Bernalillo, NM 87004
(505) 867-5351
www.nmmonuments.org/
coronado

The circular ruins of Tyuonyi Pueblo, in Bandelier National Monument, once housed hundreds of people.

Below: Ancestral Pueblo people dug many cliff houses from the weathered sandstone at Bandelier, including these dwellings at Long House.

» Bandelier National
Monument
15 Entrance Road
Los Alamos, NM 87544
(505) 672-3861
www.nps.gov/band

Archaeologists have since identified archaic campsites, field houses, kivas, cliff and cave dwellings, virtually the entire range of architectural forms of the ancient Southwest, covering thousands of years.

Bandelier could do nothing but note their presence and clamber about the rocks, taking note of Clovis points, foundation walls, and other artifacts. Later generations of scholars have explored what is called the Pajarito Plateau and its archaeological wealth, which was especially abundant from the late 1200s, a time that saw the establishment of villages containing as many as 600 rooms. The area was heavily populated until about 1500, just before the Spanish arrival. That is when descendants of its ancient inhabit-

ants founded nearby San Ildefonso, Cochiti, Santa Clara, and Kewa (formerly Santo Domingo) pueblos.

Visitors to Bandelier National Monument, one of the premier archaeological destinations in the Southwest, have a number of itineraries available to them. A couple of hours' exploration covers the museum at the visitor center and the nearby circular ruins of Tyuonyi Pueblo. A trail continues to cavate dwellings and Alcove House (formerly known as Ceremonial Cave), reached by ladders that are not for those inclined to vertigo, and to other shelters dug by hand from the crumbling cliff face. Numerous guided tours are available; check the monument's web site for more information. More ambitious visits to the 33,677-acre (13,629 ha) monument require hikes lasting a day or two round-trip over seventy miles (113 km) of trail.

PUYÉ CLIFF DWELLINGS
» *Ancestral Pueblo Culture*
A few miles north of Bandelier, and about thirty miles (48 km) north of Santa Fe, stand the Puyé Cliff Dwellings. These contain both a mesa-top village and, below it, multistory cliff houses that run about a mile (1.6 km) along a wide canyon, an altogether striking sight. Ancestral Pueblo people dug these cliff houses out of weathered volcanic rock, a laborious process, and then fronted them

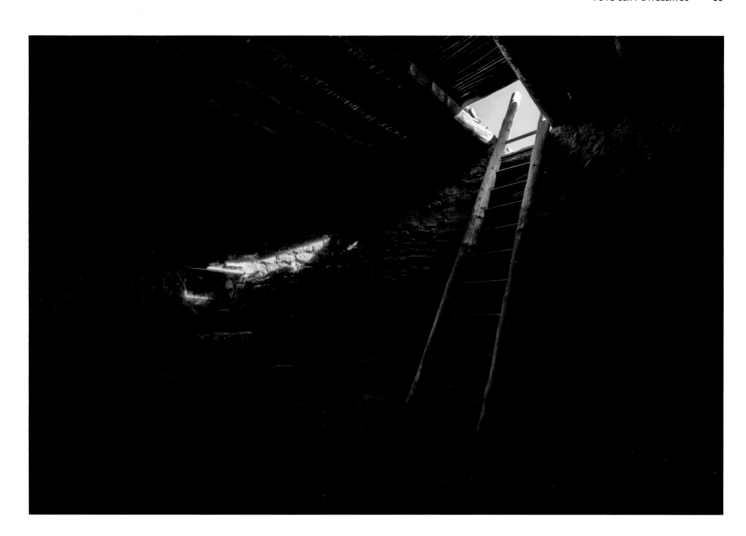

with masonry walls. Atop the cliff stands the ruin of an extensive pueblo of more than 740 rooms, anchored by a great kiva.

Puyé, a National Historic Landmark whose name means "where the rabbits gather" in Tewa, is one of the last Ancestral Pueblo villages to have been built, begun by refugees from the Mesa Verde region sometime around 1300. The settlement was the largest on the Pajarito Plateau, with a population of about two thousand. It was inhabited until about 1600, well after Europeans arrived in the region.

The ruins lie within the Santa Clara Pueblo Indian Reservation, and the Santa Clara Pueblo people consider the people of Puyé to be their direct ancestors. The Pueblo offers guided tours of the site. Check in at the visitor center before proceeding to the ruins, which lie several miles to the west along a scenic highway with sweeping views of the surrounding countryside. Be sure to visit Santa Clara Pueblo, renowned for its distinctive pottery.

Top: The Great Kiva at the Puyé Cliff Dwellings.
Above: The pueblo at Puyé contained more than 740 rooms, making it the largest on the Pajarito Plateau.

» Puyé Cliff Dwellings
Santa Clara Canyon Road
Española, NM 87532
(888) 320-5008
www.puyecliffs.com

The fourteenth-century village at Jemez stands in a strategic location above the Rio Grande Valley.

Right: The Rio Guadalupe tumbles toward the Jemez River, joining it near the modern-day Jemez Pueblo.

» Jemez Historic Site
 Highway 4
 Jemez Springs, NM 87025
 www.nmhistoricsites.org/
 jemez

JEMEZ HISTORIC SITE
» *Ancestral Pueblo Culture*

Jemez Historic Site is a National Historic Landmark that preserves a village founded in the fourteenth century, during the Pueblo IV period, by the ancestors of the modern Pueblo of Jemez people. Called Gíusewa by those descendants, the pueblo stands among the beautiful scenery of the Jemez Mountains above the Rio Grande Valley. The site covers seven acres (2.8 ha), with an interpretive trail and a visitor center that presents the pueblo's history from the perspective of the Jemez people. In addition, the surrounding area contains several well-maintained hiking trails that afford superb views of the ruins and mountains.

In 1621, Franciscan priests established a large mission at the pueblo but may have maintained it only until 1639. The ruins of the church, with its unusual octagonal bell tower, still stand, built atop part of the old village. Jemez people lived in the pueblo for another forty years, and then vacated Gíusewa during the Pueblo Revolt of 1680. Jemez National Historic Landmark lies about twenty miles (32 km) north of metropolitan Albuquerque on New Mexico Highway 4, just past the village of Jemez Springs, a favorite destination of hot spring enthusiasts.

PECOS NATIONAL HISTORICAL PARK

» Ancestral Pueblo Culture and Others

Located about twenty-five miles (40 km) east of Santa Fe, Pecos National Historical Park stands at a crossroads between the Ancestral Puebloans and other peoples of the Southwest and the Great Plains to the north and east, with whom the people of Pecos traded extensively, exchanging turquoise jewelry, for instance, for bison hides.

The park lies in the upper reaches of the Pecos River Valley, which forms an avenue all the way south through what is now West Texas and on to Mexico. The area surrounding the park contains the ruins of several structures that date to about 800 CE, though the main feature of the park proper, the red-walled Pecos Pueblo, was first built in about 1100. Over the next three hundred years, the village evolved, eventually reaching a population of about two thousand. Comprising structures called North Pueblo and South Pueblo, the village also contained numerous kivas, and a low wall surrounded the entire town. The site of Pecos was still inhabited when the Coronado Expedition passed by in 1540 and half a century

later, when another Spanish conquistador described it as containing buildings that were four or five stories tall, reached by a network of ladders from rooftop to rooftop. The Spanish established a mission church here in 1625, but it was burned down during the Pueblo Revolt of 1680. Another church, visible today, rose in its place after the Spanish returned in 1692.

The pueblo became a National Historical Park in 1990, when it acquired a nearby historic ranch as well as the Glorieta Battlefield, the site of the westernmost major battle of the Civil War.

The great kiva at Pecos Pueblo was built around 1100. Below: A low wall surrounds the great kiva at Pecos Pueblo, which was still inhabited when the first Spanish conquistadors passed by in the sixteenth century.

» Pecos National
 Historical Park
 P.O. Box 418
 Pecos, NM 87552
 (505) 757–7200
 www.nps.gov/peco

Carving of a mountain lion found at Abo, another pueblo in Salinas Pueblo Missions National Monument.

» Salinas Pueblo Missions
National Monument
102 South Ripley
Mountainair, NM 87036
(505) 847-2585
www.nps.gov/sapu

SALINAS PUEBLO MISSIONS NATIONAL MONUMENT

» Ancestral Pueblo Culture and Others

The Estancia Basin lies to the east of the Rio Grande, flanked by the tall Manzano Mountains to the west and rugged fingers of the Chupadera Mesa to the south. Also to the south lies the historic territory of the Jornada Mogollon people, exemplified by the Three Rivers Petroglyph Site (see pages 52–53), with whom the early Tiwa, Tompiro, and Jumano inhabitants of the area traded, as well as with the plains Jumano, Apache, and others. About fourteen hundred years ago, the Estancia Basin began to see the formation of small pithouse villages, succeeded, four centuries later, by surface pueblos that show some—but only some—influence from distant Chaco Canyon.

These pueblos—Abo, Gran Quivira (originally called Las Humanas), and Quarai—were well-populated. Located about eighty miles (130 km) southeast of present-day Albuquerque, they stood on the Ancestral Pueblo frontier, though they were apparently important enough that immigrants from Mesa Verde came to live among the people of the Estancia Basin after 1300. Their descendants were still occupying the pueblos when the Spanish arrived and established mission churches, but around the time of the Pueblo Revolt of 1680 the area was largely vacated. In 1909, Las Humanas became Gran Quivira National Monument, and in 1980 Abo and Quari were transferred from the State of New Mexico to form Salinas National Monument. That name was changed again in 1988 to Salinas Pueblo Missions National Monument to give equal importance to each phase of the park's history. All three units lie close to salinas, or ancient salt flats.

Each unit of the monument has a small visitor center, while, in the handsome small town of Mountainair, the monument as a whole has a central visitor center with a museum. Visiting the main center and walking the interpretive trails at the three pueblos will take the better part of a day.

Top: Gran Quivira, one of three pueblos in the Salinas Pueblo Missions National Monument, lies on the eastern frontier of the Ancestral Pueblo world. It was inhabited until about 1680. Opposite: Abo Pueblo, one of the three large pueblos protected within Salinas Pueblo Missions National Monument, was an important trading center between the plains to the east and settlements along the Rio Grande to the west.

UTAH

HOVENWEEP NATIONAL MONUMENT

» Ancestral Pueblo Culture

People have been living in the vicinity of what is now Hovenweep National Monument, on the border of southwestern Colorado and southeastern Utah, for a very long time—at least ten thousand years, judging from campsites dating to the Paleoindian era and, later, the first blossoming of the Basketmaker Culture. Occupied nearly continuously until about six hundred years ago, Hovenweep unquestionably qualifies as one of the most ancient settlements on the North American continent.

Cajon Mesa, along which Hovenweep National Monument runs for sixteen miles (26 km), had been long vacated by the time Navajo and Ute people moved into the area,

and indigenous guides warned the Anglo explorers who came to the area in the 1850s that the ruins there were inhabited by ghosts. That view is certainly understandable, for at many times of the year the vast sprawl of Hovenweep seems to be without humans at all, lending support to the name of the place, which means "desolate valley" in the Ute language.

A thousand years ago, however, Hovenweep was a flourishing, busy place. In about 950, when nearby Mesa Verde was being developed, the inhabitants of the area began to move from their individual houses to newly built pueblos. Some, such as the unit called the Cajon Group, were relatively small, whereas others, such as the Cutthroat Castle group, may have sheltered a

Above: This sandal worn by an Ancestral Puebloan long ago is now housed at Edge of the Cedars State Park.

Opposite: Holly Tower and Holly House, located at the head of Keeley Canyon, are two of the imposing structures within one of the five outlying units at Hovenweep National Monument.

Tower Point Ruin looks out onto Little Ruin Canyon and snow-covered Ute Mountain in the distance. Within a short distance stand several other major structures, including Hovenweep Castle and Square Tower.

Hovenweep Castle, the namesake of Hovenweep National Monument, is one of the largest structures on Cajon Mesa. The Ute name Hovenweep means "desolate valley."

Opposite: House of Fire Ruin, located on Cedar Mesa near Blanding, Utah, takes its name from the spectacularly weathered sandstone formation that lies above it.

» Hovenweep
   National Monument
   McElmo Route
   Cortez, CO 81321
   (970) 562–4282 ext. 10
   www.nps.gov/hove/index.
   htm

few hundred people in numerous buildings. That cluster of buildings stands in the open, unlike other groups in Hovenweep, which are tucked away at the heads of canyons. That location, along with its large number of kivas, leads some to believe that Cut-throat Castle may have been the ceremonial heart of the area.

The largest structures among the six villages within the monument are in the Square Tower group, which may have held five hundred people from about 1200 to some time before 1300. The Square Tower itself is three stories tall, made of tightly fitted stones. Hovenweep Castle, within the same group, is similarly impressive, and it is aligned so that openings in its walls project light from each solstice and equinox.

An easy loop trail, about two miles (3.2 km) long, starts from the visitor center and leads to the edge of a steep-walled canyon and the pueblo called Stronghold House. Trails of varying degrees of difficulty lead to the outlying pueblos. Those who come to this comparatively little-traveled area, with its structures scattered across a vast and striking landscape, will find that it affords a rich view of the ancient Pueblo past.

CEDAR MESA AND NATURAL BRIDGES NATIONAL MONUMENT

» *Ancestral Pueblo Culture and Others*

Lying northwest of Hovenweep, Cedar Mesa is an ancient reef that rises like a tree-clad island from the desert floor below. The plateau is vast, covering an area of nearly four hundred square miles (1,036 sq km), and the rugged wilderness is a popular destination for campers and hikers today.

As with many other Ancestral Pueblo settlements, the people who first made their homes on Cedar Mesa first lived in pithouses, and then, many centuries later, moved to structures under rock overhangs and high atop cliffs lining the mesa's narrow, steep canyons. Though difficult to reach, those cliff houses lay close to mesa-top gardens and fields that were intensively worked, even as the Ancestral Pueblo people fanned out across the territory to hunt game and gather wild foods.

Many sites in Cedar Mesa are quite accessible. One is Mule Canyon Ruin, a twelve-room surface pueblo built about seven hundred years ago. The ruin includes a kiva and a tower, both of which have been stabilized; a canopy protects the kiva. That site lies near

Moon House Ruin is one of the most interesting Ancestral Pueblo sites found in southeastern Utah's Cedar Mesa.

Below: The Horsecollar Ruins are among the well-preserved ancient structures hidden in Natural Bridges National Monument.

» U.S. Bureau of
Land Management
Monticello Field Office
365 North Main
Monticello, Utah 84535
(435) 587–1500
www.blm.gov/ut/st/en/fo/
monticello/recreation/
places/cedar_mesa.html

Highway 95, has a paved parking area, and is open year-round without restriction. Mule Canyon also contains the House of Fire Ruin, which takes its name from the curious sunburst effect that water meeting the oxidized patina called "desert varnish" has made over countless millennia. Getting to it requires only a 1.5-mile (2.4 km) hike, and it sees many visitors. The Fallen Ceiling (or Fallen Roof) Ruin, a small four-room pueblo in Road Canyon whose collapsed cave ceiling gives it its name, calls for more walking and route-finding, but it's still a relatively easy trip.

Some ruins on Cedar Mesa are restricted. Moon House Ruin, for instance, which lies in McLoyd Canyon, is limited to twenty visitors a day (though it often sees nowhere near as many). Individuals are required to sign in at the Kane Gulch Ranger Station, and the Bureau of Land Management warns that the one-mile hike to the site is rough and "not for those who fear heights."

The curiously round Horsecollar Ruins are located in an area of the mesa designated as Natural Bridges National Monument. Preserving three large natural arches, the monument also contains several other Ancestral Pueblo ruins. Though known to local Ute, Paiute, and Navajo people, those ruins were officially "discovered" only in the twentieth century, and they were in unusually good shape, because their remoteness meant that no one had stripped them of building materials or remains. The man who first described them, a rancher named Zeke Johnson, recounted that he found abundant broken pottery and flaked stone at the site, indicating a long settlement. He ruefully admitted to feeling like "a foolish kid" for having lived in the area so long and not having known of the ruins' existence, but he noted appreciatively that, despite signs that other visitors had come before him, all who had come to the site had left the remains alone—a rarity, given how many ancient sites were plundered in the past.

Natural Bridges National Monument (www.nps.gov/nabr), the first officially designated national monument in Utah, contains several extraordinary rock-art panels, including numerous handprints of the artists and perhaps their families, desert bighorn sheep, and the horned, ghostly figures that archaeologists call "anthropomorphs," meaning "of human form."

COMB RIDGE
» Ancestral Pueblo Culture

Lying alongside Cedar Mesa is eighty-mile (129 km)-long Comb Ridge, another ancient reef that runs roughly north–south into northeastern Arizona. Designated a National Natural Landmark, the ridge is tall and sheer, which did not deter the Ancestral Pueblo people from digging shallow handholds and footholds called "Moki steps" into the cliff face, paving a decidedly challenging way to get to cliff dwellings such as Monarch Cave Ruin. Some of these cliff dwellings contain artifacts such as potsherds and stone knives. Others contain fine examples of rock art, such as the intricate grouping called the Procession Panel, dating back many hundreds of years.

On the east side of Comb Ridge lies Butler Wash, site of the Butler Wash Ruins, a cliff dwelling that was built by Ancestral Pueblo people in about 1200. Parts of the ruins have been rebuilt and stabilized and reconstructed, but most of it remains just as it was found in the mid-1800s. Along with dwellings and granaries, the site contains four kivas. A trail leads to an overlook that

Discovered by hikers in the 1980s, the Procession Panel, a site on Comb Ridge, Utah, is a splendid example of prehistoric rock art. Below: Ancestral Pueblo settlers built the cliff dwellings called the Butler Wash Ruins in about 1200.

allows visitors to take in this splendid site. The trail winds over slickrock and difficult terrain, and even though it is only about a mile long, visitors should allow plenty of time to follow it to the vista.

» Comb Ridge
http://bluffutah.org/comb-ridge/

Five Petroglyph and Pictograph Sites
» *Ancestral Pueblo Culture and Others*

Buckhorn Wash Rock Art Panel. Located in east-central Utah about sixty miles (97 km) west of Arches National Park, the San Rafael Swell is a dome-shaped mass of rock that has been deformed and eroded into complex folds and deep canyons. Interstate 70 bisects the San Rafael Swell and is the only paved road to provide access to it. Humans have never been plentiful in this austere country, which is otherworldly enough to have served as a filming location for the 2009 film *Star Trek*, but those who did live here left an extraordinary body of rock art over the centuries. On the walls of Buckhorn Wash (on some maps, called Buckhorn Draw), about two thousand years ago, those painters dabbed red paint made of powdered hematite and albumen and recorded what they saw all around them: animals, people, plants, stars. The pictographic panel spans more than 130 feet (40 m) and is testimonial to the talents of a little-known people called the Barrier Canyon Culture.

www.emerycounty.com/Travel/san-rafael-swell-buckhorn-wash-rock-art-panel.html

Sego Canyon Rock Art Site. Another Barrier Canyon Culture site, Sego Canyon also contains rock paintings by members of the ancient Fremont Culture and by historic Ute Indians. Though just a few miles north of busy Interstate 70, the site lies in remote and rugged country, but it is not difficult to reach, thanks to a paved road that leads to a nearby parking area with interpretive plaques and even a restroom. Sego Canyon also contains a ghost town and abandoned mine.

www.blm.gov/ut/st/en/prog/more/cultural/archaeology/places_to_visit/sego_canyon.html

Newspaper Rock State Historic Monument. Lying along the main road into the Needles District of Canyonlands National Park, about twelve miles (19 km) west of US 191 between Monticello and Moab, Newspaper Rock is one of the most extensive petroglyph sites in Utah. It contains rock art by numerous cultures: Archaic, Fremont, Ancestral Pueblo, and Navajo. Altogether, the sandstone cliff that lends the site its name contains more than 650 images. The name of the cliff in Navajo is "Tse' Honé," meaning "rock that tells a story"—and this fascinating site tells many, including the arrival of Europeans in the region, as evidenced by the horses found on several panels.

www.blm.gov/ut/st/en/prog/more/cultural/archaeology/places_to_visit/Newspaper_Rock.html

Dry Fork Canyon Rock Art Site. Located near Dinosaur National Monument, Dry Fork Canyon lies on private ranchland whose owners generously allow the public to visit without charge. (Donations are welcome, though.) The trail from the parking area to the site is steep and rock-strewn, but the effort is repaid by an extraordinary sequence of both petroglyphs and pictographs, hundreds of them, some as large as nine feet (2.7 m) tall. Most images are from people of the Fremont Culture, who made them more than a thousand years ago.

www.utah.com/vernal/dryforkcanyonrockart. htm

Nine Mile Canyon Petroglyph Site. Located in northeastern Utah, Nine Mile Canyon is in truth some forty miles (64 km) long. The canyon houses more than a thousand individual rock art sites, most made by people of the Fremont Culture, and more than ten thousand images have been catalogued there. The wealth of images and sites here, as well as other archaeological evidence, has led scholars to regard Nine Mile Canyon as one of the most important centers of the Fremont people, and it was inhabited for some three hundred years, from about 950 CE to about 1250 CE.

www.blm.gov/ut/st/en/fo/vernal/recreation_/ nine_mile_canyon.html

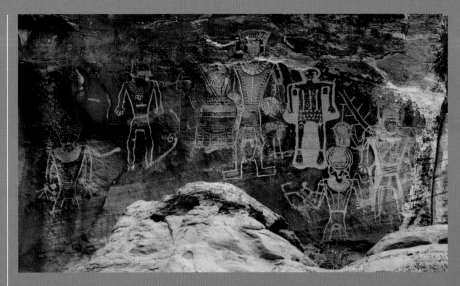

Reading Rock Art

A circle. A bighorn sheep? Multi-pointed geometrical shapes. A lizard? A projectile point?

The ancient peoples of the Southwest left behind thousands of rock carvings (petroglyphs) and paintings (pictographs) with these and countless other forms. Few ancient settlements are without such artwork, suggesting that making images was an important form of expression. But what do they mean? The possibilities for interpretation of those forms are endless. Polly Schaafsma, an archaeologist and authority on Southwestern rock art, notes that a four-pointed star can variously represent a rain-bringing katsina, the planet Venus, or the Aztec god Quetzalcoatl. It may even speak to a war-related ceremony, for the planets can be symbols of conflict as well as of life. Many modern Native peoples discern the clan symbols of their ancestors in the rock art, and a large body of scholarship has grown around the subject.

Petroglyph sites serve many purposes as well. They are places that enshrine ancient aspirations (may we have a good hunt, may there be plenty of water for us and the animals we chase) and observations (these are the kinds of animals we see in this place, this is what a storm looks like). They mark boundaries, point to water and the stars, and chronicle the movement of herds of animals and groups of people over centuries. As you visit archaeological sites, pay close attention to these symbols from the ancient past.

Anthropomorphs at McKee Springs,
Dinosaur National Monument, Utah.

DINOSAUR NATIONAL MONUMENT
» Fremont Culture

Dinosaur National Monument contains the remains of more than the ancient reptiles who give it its name. Within the 210,000 acres (85,000 ha) of the monument, located on the border of Utah and Colorado, lie some majestic examples of Fremont Culture rock art, most of them petroglyphs. The Tour of the Tilted Rocks, a loop drive that covers only ten miles (16 km) but takes two hours to drive (without stops), leads to several panels that include images of one of the Fremont people's favorite subjects: the abundant lizards that sun in this rocky place, and which provided a ready source of food. One lizard glyph is impressively large, some six feet (1.8 m) long and carved twenty feet (6 m) above the ground. Some petroglyph sites, such as the Deluge Shelter, require travel by four-wheel-drive vehicle or a substantial hike. One that formerly did, the McKee site, is now served by a good gravel road.

» Dinosaur National
  Monument
  4545 U.S. 40
  Dinosaur, CO 81610
  (435) 781–7700
  www.nps.gov/dino

As befits the name of the place, many large rock art representations of lizards can be found at Cub Creek within Dinosaur National Monument.

CANYONLANDS NATIONAL PARK AND ARCHES NATIONAL PARK

» *Ancestral Pueblo Culture and Others*

Canyonlands National Park, located near Moab, comprises more than a third of a million acres (134,000 ha). It is a celebration of geology and the power of water to cut through stone. And even though it sees some half a million visitors each year, it is so vast, and so much of it remote, that it seems nearly deserted. Yet, throughout that vast loneliness, thousands of archaeological sites have been catalogued, some belonging to the so-called Archaic people who came into the area more than seven thousand years ago, some to the Ancestral Pueblo people who built small settlements about a thousand years ago. It is possible that outlier groups of people from the Fremont Culture, who were mostly concentrated well to the north of Canyonlands, settled in the area as well.

Two accessible archaeological sites are Roadside Ruin and Tower Ruin, both found near the Needles Visitor Center. Horseshoe Canyon, once called Barrier Canyon (and thus being the namesake for the Barrier

Top: An intricately rendered pictograph at the Great Gallery, Canyonlands National Park. Below: False Kiva, a circular structure whose date has not been pinpointed, is one of the many spectacular, and remote, treasures within Canyonlands.

» Canyonlands National Park
   2282 Resource Boulevard
   Moab, UT 84532
   (435) 719–2313
   www.nps.gov/cany

» Arches National Park
   N Highway 191
   Moab, UT 84532
   (435) 719–2299
   www.nps.gov/arch

A storm brews behind Edge of the Cedars Pueblo, Utah, an Ancestral Pueblo village that was inhabited for three to four centuries beginning in about 825.

Canyon Culture, the people who made the Buckhorn Wash Rock Art Panel, described on page 74), contains haunting pictographs of ghostlike figures that some have interpreted as supernatural beings. Nearby Arches National Park contains comparatively few archaeological sites, though it has some notable rock art by Ancestral Pueblo, Fremont, and Ute hands. This paucity suggests that, as today, more people came to behold the wonderland of stone than to live there.

Interestingly, a village called Site 13 near Canyonlands, dating to the end of the 700s, turns up the first evidence north of Mexico of the use of chocolate. Given that cacao comes from the Mesoamerican tropics thousands of miles away, this finding is evidence, once again, of how extensive the trade was between the Southwest and southern Mexico.

EDGE OF THE CEDARS STATE PARK
» *Ancestral Pueblo Culture*

Edge of the Cedars State Park, located just outside Blanding, preserves a sizeable Ancestral Pueblo site containing a village that was inhabited from about 825 CE to about 1225 CE. The earliest structures were pithouses that in time evolved into the surface pueblo whose remains stand here today. Only a very small portion of that village is visible, for most of it has yet to be excavated, a project reserved for future generations of archaeologists.

The park was named to the National Register of Historic Places in 1971. It takes its name from the fact that the village stands near a large forest of juniper trees, which Mormon settlers called cedars. The forest sheltered abundant wildlife and provided building materials and fuel,

The Edge of the Cedars State Park contains an important museum devoted to Ancestral Pueblo Culture, with artifacts such as this atlatl dart tool kit. The stone dart is attached to a wooden shaft, then thrown with a carved piece of wood that serves as an arm extension.

MONUMENT VALLEY NAVAJO TRIBAL PARK AND MYSTERY VALLEY

» Ancestral Pueblo Culture and Others

The presence of humans in Monument Valley, a haunting landscape of weathered mesas, cliffs, and rock spires, dates back as long as twelve thousand years—and perhaps even earlier. The valley, which extends south into Arizona, became an early home to the Ancestral Pueblo people, who established villages of pithouses, then surface pueblos, and then cliff dwellings whose remains dot the area. A seventeen-mile (27 km)-long loop road gives visitors an overview of the area, but to see these ruins and their associated rock art panels—perhaps best known of them the "leaping sheep" glyph at Eye of the Sun Arch—up close, you will need to hire a Navajo guide.

The Monument Valley Navajo Tribal Park lies just south of the Utah border in northeastern Arizona. Check in at the visitor center there before proceeding into the park by way of the loop road. The valley beyond the visitor center contains numerous natural arches in the sandstone, including Needle Eye Arch (also called the Eye of

making it an attractive place to settle in ancient times—and an attractive place to visit today. An onsite museum contains a large, comprehensive collection of pottery and other Ancestral Pueblo artifacts. The Grand Gulch area, which contains features with such resonant names as Perfect Kiva, is even more remote, and visitors must obtain a backcountry permit from the Bureau of Land Management.

Above: Mancos ceramic ladles at Edge of the Cedars State Park.

Right: The House of Many Hands is a deeply hidden site in Mystery Valley, which lies adjacent to Monument Valley, on the Utah-Arizona border.

» Edge of the Cedars State Park
PO Box 788
Blanding, UT 84511
(435) 678-2238
www.stateparks.utah.gov/
park/edge-of-the-cedars-
state-park-museum

the Rabbit) and Skull Arch. One of its most impressive archaeological sites is the Square House Ruin, which takes some effort to get to, perched as it is high within a sandstone alcove. The builders of the ruin took care to make the exterior walls especially smooth, evidence of both their advanced building skills and the importance of the site. To the right of the ruin are several depictions of bighorn sheep, while along the valley floor below are numerous other petroglyphs. A nearby side canyon houses Baby House (or Baby Feet) Ruins, so called because handprints and footprints carved on the floor of this structure, probably used for storage, appear to be baby-sized. Deeper within Mystery Valley, an area adjacent to Monument Valley, is another Ancestral Pueblo site called the House of Many Hands, which owes its name to the numerous handprints visible on the rock walls.

For information about guides within the tribal park, call Goulding's Lodge at (435) 727-3231 or the new The View Hotel at (435) 727-5555, or visit http://navajonationparks.org/htm/monumentvalleytours.htm.

A pictograph at the Many Hands Ruin site in Monument Valley Tribal Park depicts anthropomorphic, or human-form, figures.

Above: The famed "leaping sheep" glyph at Eye of the Sun Arch in Monument Valley is among the best-known examples of ancient rock art in the Southwest.

Pages 82–83: Square House Ruin sits in a deep rock alcove that helps conceal it from view. Even hidden away, it opens onto the incomparable grandeur of Mystery Valley and, beyond it, Monument Valley, among the hallmark landscapes of the Southwest.

Monument Valley
Navajo Tribal Park
PO Box 360289
Monument Valley, UT 84536
(435) 727-5874
http://navajonationparks.org/htm/monumentvalley.htm

Glossary

Anasazi *See Ancestral Pueblo people.*

Ancestral Pueblo people Formerly known as the Anasazi, a Navajo word meaning "ancestors of our enemy," the Ancestral Pueblo people were an ancient people of the Colorado Plateau region. Their early culture probably included migrants from Mesoamerica as well as descendants of the Basketmaker people. The descendants of the Ancestral Pueblo people include the Hopi, Zuni, Acoma, Santa Clara, and many other modern Pueblo groups.

ballcourt An import from Mesoamerica, ballcourts were features of Hohokam and Sinagua civilization from about 750 CE to 1200 CE; about two hundred have been identified at Hohokam sites. Oval in shape, most ballcourts were about a hundred feet (30 m) in length. A goal at each end accommodated a rubber or rock ball. The ballcourts probably served ceremonial and political functions beyond mere entertainment.

Basketmaker When Richard Wetherill, a rancher and trader, first explored early Ancestral Pueblo sites on the Colorado Plateau in the 1880s, he found numerous finely woven baskets of fiber and reed of the kind shown to the right. He called the people who made them "Basket Makers." The designation has since been applied to Ancestral Pueblo Culture up to 700 CE. Most modern archaeologists call the Basketmaker I phase the Late Archaic.

big houses During the Classic Period (1150–1450 CE), Hohokam builders erected numerous multistoried adobe towers atop platform mounds. The best known of these "big houses" today is Casa Grande (see pages 13–15). Archaeologists believe that other big houses were even larger.

Clovis Culture The Paleoindian Clovis Culture, which emerged at about 11,500 BCE, was widespread in what is now the Southwest. Once thought to be the earliest people in the Americas, the Clovis Culture is distinguished by sharply fluted projectile weapons called Clovis points.

dendrochronology The scientific study of tree rings. It is among several scientific techniques archaeologists use to date the age of wooden beams and other materials, and thus to narrow down the time at which a particular site was built.

Folsom Culture Following on the Clovis tradition, a group of hunting peoples who flourished in the Southwest from about 9500 BCE to 8000 BCE.

Fremont Culture Thought to be ancestors of Great Basin peoples such as the Ute and Shoshone, the Fremont Culture developed contemporaneously with the Ancestral Pueblo Culture. The Fremont people lived to the north and west of the Pueblo heartland, leaving intricate works of rock art as far north as what is now Wyoming and as far west as Nevada.

great houses Large structures that are numerous in Chaco Canyon. Some contained as many as seven hundred rooms, with numerous kivas in a rough ratio of one kiva for every thirty rooms. Nine Chaco great houses also had oversized "great kivas," the largest sixty-three feet (19 m) in diameter.

Hohokam The Hohokam Culture arose in what is now central and southern Arizona, with its most notable settlements lying along the Gila River and its tributaries, especially the Salt and Santa Cruz rivers. Archaeologists put the emergence of a distinctive Hohokam Culture at about 1 CE.

kiva Evolving from the subterranean structure called the pithouse, the kiva was an enclosed room, built partly or wholly underground, that served numerous functions, especially ceremonial, among the Ancestral Pueblo people.

lithics In archaeology, shaped stone tools such as knives or scrapers for removing animal skin. A lithic assemblage is a grouping of such tools.

mano From the Spanish word for "hand," a mano is a grinding stone that can be held with one or two hands and used to mill grain with an accompanying metate.

Mesoamerica The area designated by archaeologists from northern Costa Rica to central Mexico, embracing the homelands of the Maya and Aztec civilizations. Many cultures in the ancient Southwest had contacts with Mesoamerica, mostly its northern reaches, and numerous influences from Mesoamerica can be seen in their artifacts.

metate A flat or recessed oblong stone (see the image to the right) on which grain is placed and then ground with a smaller stone called a mano.

midden An archaeological term for a garbage heap containing the remains of food, broken pottery and tools, and other materials. Material recovered from middens is often the best indicator of how a given people lived.

Mogollon Descendants of the ancient Cochise Culture who made their homes in the highlands of northern Mexico, southwestern New Mexico, and southeastern Arizona. An outlier group, the Jornada Mogollon, lived east of the Rio Grande, but the best-known Mogollon group in the Southwest is the Mimbres people of the upper Gila and Mimbres River valleys.

petroglyph A kind of rock art made by engraving or carving into stone.

pictograph A painting on rock. In some instances in the Southwest, both pictographs and petroglyphs can be found at the same site.

pithouse Throughout the Southwest, early people lived in pithouses, which were generally oval areas dug into the ground to a depth of a few feet and then covered over with branches, reeds, dirt, or other roofing material. Pithouses eventually gave way to aboveground structures accompanied by descendant structures called kivas.

platform mound Early platform mounds, which were common in the Hohokam cultural area and other parts of the Southwest, were small, low circular berms. By the Classic Period, beginning in about 1150 CE, these mounds were large rectangles. One of the largest was built at Pueblo Grande (see pages 15–16), measuring 160 by 294 feet (49 by 90 m) and rising to a height of thirty feet (9 m). The mounds may have served as defenses and had ceremonial functions, but they also may have provided residences for elites.

pottery A range of shaped and baked ceramic vessels that is an important indicator of the presence of people at a given site. Because it is fragile and less portable than baskets or hide containers, pottery is associated with permanent settlements.

projectile point In archaeological terms, a shaped weapon of stone, obsidian, or other material that is fitted to a shaft, such as a spear or arrow. Differences in projectile points distinguish the prehistoric Clovis and Folsom Cultures.

pueblo From the Spanish word meaning "town," a multistoried building, usually made of adobe and timber, containing anywhere from a few rooms to many hundreds of them. The house form evolved from earlier pithouses more than a thousand years ago.

Salado The Salado people lived in the Tonto Basin of eastern Arizona and surrounding areas, flourishing in the thirteenth century CE, when their distinctive polychrome pottery style emerged. Some archaeologists consider the Salado to be an outlier Hohokam group that absorbed Mogollon and Ancestral Pueblo traditions.

Sinagua A prehistoric group who lived in Arizona between the Verde River Valley northward to the high plateau below the Grand Canyon. They flourished as a distinctive culture from about 500 CE to about 1425 CE.

Museums with Major Prehistoric Southwestern Collections

ARIZONA

Amerind Museum
2100 N. Amerind Road
Dragoon, AZ 85609
(520) 586-3666
www.amerind.org
An important museum and research center for cultures throughout the core Southwest and northern Mexico.

Arizona Museum of Natural History
53 North MacDonald
Mesa, AZ 85201
(480) 644-2230
www.azmnh.org
A general collection representing Southwestern cultures, especially the Hohokam.

Arizona State Museum
University of Arizona
Tucson, AZ 85721
(520) 621-6302
www.statemuseum.arizona.edu
A general collection embracing many Southwestern cultures.

Museum of Northern Arizona
3101 North Fort Valley Road
Flagstaff, AZ 86001
(928) 774-5213
www.musnaz.org
An important regional museum, especially for the Sinagua Culture.

Pueblo Grande Museum and Archaeological Park
4619 East Washington Street
Phoenix, AZ 85034
(602) 495-0901
www.pueblogrande.com
Please see pages 15–16.

CALIFORNIA

Southwest Museum
4700 Western Heritage Way
Los Angeles, CA 90027-1462
(323) 667-2000
http://theautry.org/exhibitions/highlights-of-the-southwest-museum-collection
A general collection, with particular attention to the ancient peoples of California.

COLORADO

Crow Canyon Archaeological Center
23390 Road K
Cortez, CO 81321–9408
(970) 565–8975
www.crowcanyon.org
Please see page 46.

Denver Museum of Nature and Science
2001 Colorado Boulevard
Denver, CO 80205
(303) 322-7009
www.dmns.org
A general collection, including Ancestral Pueblo and Fremont material.

ILLINOIS

Field Museum of Natural History
1400 South Lake Shore Drive
Chicago, IL 60605-2496
(312) 922-9410
www.fieldmuseum.org
One of the most important anthropological collections in the United States, containing many Southwestern artifacts.

MASSACHUSETTS

Peabody Museum of Archaeology and Ethnology
Harvard University
11 Divinity Avenue
Cambridge, MA 02138
www.peabody.harvard.edu
An important repository, especially of Ancestral Pueblo, Sinagua, and Mogollon materials gathered by nineteenth- and early twentieth-century archaeological expeditions.

NEVADA

Nevada State Museum
309 S. Valley View Boulevard
Las Vegas, NV 89107
(702) 486-5205
www.museums.nevadaculture.org
Contains material from southern Nevada and neighboring regions, including some Fremont holdings.

NEW MEXICO

Deming Luna Mimbres Museum
301 South Silver Ave
Deming, NM 88030
(575) 546–2382
www.lunacountyhistoricalsociety.com
A small museum containing splendid
examples of Mimbres Mogollon pottery.

Indian Pueblo Cultural Center
2401 12th Street NW
Albuquerque, NM 87104
(866) 855-7902
www.indianpueblo.org
A major collection of Ancestral Pueblo
and modern Pueblo material culture.

Maxwell Museum of Anthropology
1 University Boulevard NE
Albuquerque, NM 87131
(505) 277-4405
www.unm.edu/~maxwell
One of the most extensive anthropological museums in the United States,
with extensive materials from throughout the Southwest.

Museum of Indian Arts and Culture/
Laboratory of Anthropology
710 Camino Lejo
Santa Fe, NM 87504
(505) 476-1250
www.miaclab.org
Contains materials from throughout
the Southwest.

New Mexico State University Museum
Kent Hall, MSC 3564
P.O. Box 30001
Las Cruces, NM 88003-8001
(575) 646-5161
www.nmsu.edu/museum
A regionally important museum, with
extensive Mimbres Mogollon holdings.

Western New Mexico University
Museum
1000 West College Avenue
Silver City, NM 88061
(575) 538–6386
www.wnmumuseum.org
Contains the world's most complete
collection of Mimbres Mogollon
artifacts.

NEW YORK

American Museum of Natural History
Central Park West
New York, NY 10024
(212) 769-5100
www.amnh.org
A general collection, including artifacts
taken from many major sites in the
Southwest.

TEXAS

Museum of the Southwest
1705 W. Missouri Avenue
Midland, TX 79701
(432) 683-2882
www.museumsw.org
Houses material from the eastern edge
of the Southwest, including the Mimbres Mogollon.

Witte Museum
3801 Broadway
San Antonio, TX 78209
(210) 357-1900
www.wittemuseum.org
Contains holdings from ancient cultures of the Lower Pecos River Valley,
including some Mimbres Mogollon
material.

UTAH

Edge of the Cedars State Park Museum
660 West 400 North
Blanding, UT 84511
http://stateparks.utah.gov/park/
edge-of-the-cedars-state-park-museum
(435) 678-2238
Contains the largest collection of Ancestral Puebloan pottery on display in
the Four Corners region, as well as an
actual Puebloan village.

Natural History Museum of Utah
301 Wakara Way
Salt Lake City, UT 84108
www.nhmu.utah.edu
(801) 581-4303
An extensive general collection, with
Fremont and Ancestral Pueblo material.

WASHINGTON, DC

National Museum of the
American Indian
Smithsonian Institution
4th Street & Independence Avenue SW
Washington, DC 20560
(202) 633-6644
www.nmai.si.edu
The premier general collection of Native American material in the country, with items from throughout the
Southwest.

Acknowledgments

I owe thanks to three teachers who inducted me into the world of Southwestern archaeology. At the University of Arizona, William Rathje put me to work sifting through mounds of refuse in an early iteration of his famed Garbage Project/Projet du Garbàge, while Raymond H. Thompson, then head of the Anthropology Department, set me to thinking about soil horizons and power elites. For many years, but fewer than I would have liked, I also studied informally with Julian D. Hayden, ascended master of all things Southwestern—and much more besides.

John Carpenter and Doug Craig, expert archaeologists, answered endless questions. Though in archaeology today's errors often become tomorrow's orthodoxy, John and Doug, along with Allen Dart, also helped keep today's errors from being simply tomorrow's errors. Any such errors are my own, with the proviso that in Southwestern archaeology one person's error is another person's conjecture—which explains the old joke that if you put two Southwestern archaeologists in a room together, there'll be three conflicting theories within just a few minutes.

I owe thanks as well to friends for conversations over the years that have figured in these pages, among them Edward Abbey, Keith Basso, Charles Bowden, Bill Broyles, Linda Cordell, Rose Houk, Alfonso Ortiz, Simon Ortiz, Emory Sekaquaptewa, Tom Sheridan, Daniel Staley, Christine Szuter, and Norman Yoffee.

Too many of them are gone, but I like to think that Callimachus, the Greek librarian and poet, was right when he wrote that the dead are not really dead, but fly over the sea like gulls. Or, at least in Ed's case, over the sand like turkey vultures.

GREGORY MCNAMEE

Heartfelt gratitude goes to my wife, Wendy, for her encouragement, understanding, and support while I was working on the photography for this book, and to my mother, Shirley Lindahl, for introducing me to American Indian culture and art early in my life.

A special thanks to these individuals who helped with their time and expertise: Ron Ayers, David Bowyer, Bill Crawley, Juanita Edaakie, Russell Gerbrace, Ted Grussing, Jim Hook, David Jenney, Roy Julian, Ty Lampe, Peter Pilles, Nina Rehfeld, Tallson Rocha, John Schaefer, Duane Tawahongva, Brad and Denise Traver, and Deborah Westfall.

LARRY LINDAHL

The author and photographer also extend particular appreciation to the team at Rio Nuevo Publishers: Ross Humphreys, Susan Lowell, Aaron Downey, Caroline Cook, Jim Turner, and Suzan Cousino.

For news and updates about this book and its contents, please visit www.ancientsouthwest.com.
For photographic prints and additional information please visit: www.LarryLindahl.com

Further Reading

Bahr, Donald, Juan Smith, William Smith Allison, and Julian Hayden. *The Short Swift Time of Gods on Earth: The Hohokam Chronicles.* Berkeley: University of California Press, 1994.

Booker, Margaret Moore. *Southwest Art Defined: An Illustrated Guide.* Tucson: Rio Nuevo Publishers, 2013.

Cole, Sally J. *Legacy on Stone: Rock Art of the Colorado Plateau and Four Corners Region.* Boulder, CO: Johnson Books, 1990.

Cordell, Linda S., and Maxine E. McBrinn. *Archaeology of the Southwest.* Third edition. Walnut Creek, CA: Left Coast Press, 2012.

Downum, Christian E., ed. *Hisat'sinom: Ancient Peoples in a Land without Water.* Santa Fe: SAR Press, 2012.

Farnsworth, Janet. *Rock Art Along the Way.* Tucson: Rio Nuevo Publishers, 2006.

Fish, Suzanne K., and Paul R. Fish, eds. *The Hohokam Millennium.* Santa Fe: SAR Press, 2007.

Grant, Campbell. *Canyon de Chelly: Its People and Rock Art.* Tucson: University of Arizona Press, 1978.

Kosik, Fran. *Native Roads: The Complete Motoring Guide to the Navajo and Hopi Nations.* Third edition. Tucson: Rio Nuevo Publishers, 2013.

Lowry, Joe Dan, and Joe P. Lowry. *Turquoise Unearthed.* Tucson: Rio Nuevo Publishers, 2002.

Malville, J. McKim. *A Guide to Prehistoric Astronomy in the Southwest.* Boulder, CO: Johnson Books, 2008.

Nelson, Margaret C., and Michelle Hegmon, eds. *Mimbres Lives and Landscapes.* Santa Fe: SAR Press, 2010.

Reid, Jefferson, and Stephanie Whittlesey. *The Archaeology of Ancient Arizona.* Tucson: University of Arizona Press, 1997.

Vivian, R. Gwinn, and Bruce Hilpert. *The Chaco Handbook.* Second edition. Salt Lake City: University of Utah Press, 2012.

Opposite: Macaw feathers from distant Mexico are part of an ornate sash found in Canyonlands National Park, Utah. The sash, on display at Edge of the Cedars State Park Museum, dates to about 1150.